Cyber Security Resear

Norwich University Applied Research Institutes

2017 Annual Report
Of
Top Cyber Security Incidents

Edited by:

THOMAS HYSLIP

ROSEMARIE PELLETIER

GEORGE SILOWASH

i

CONTENTS

COVER DESIGN

Jan Paolo Cruz

POW Graphix Unlimited

Janpaolocruzrn@yahoo.com

1

INTRODUCTION

While the fallout from the Russian cyber operations in the 2016 Presidential election was fresh in everyone's mind, there were many noteworthy cybersecurity incidents in 2017. Russia continued its cyber-attacks, most notably in the Ukraine and the effects were felt across the globe. We also got a look behind the curtain at the Central Intelligence Agency's cyber operations when hackers leaked the CIA's cyber techniques and tools to Wikileaks. Not to be outdone by their sister Intelligence Agency, the National Security Agency was also compromised and their tool, Eternal Blue, was used to create the WannaCry Ransomware which affected users in over 150 countries.

In total we examined 14 cybersecurity incidents that span the commercial, military and government cyberspace. As you will see, no one is immune from cyber-attacks and the old cliché still holds true, the best offense is good defense. So be sure to keep your computer systems up to date with the latest security patches and follow good cybersecurity hygiene.

Thank you for purchasing our book and supporting Norwich University. The chapter authors are all current students or graduates of Norwich University, College of Graduate and Continuing Studies, Master's Degree programs.

2

WIKILEAKS CIA VAULT 7 & 8

By: Jonathan Lancelot

The multi-edged sword of national security, cybersecurity, the 4th Amendment, espionage, and freedom of the press all come together in cyberspace in this case. "In what appeared to be the largest leak of Central Intelligence Agency (CIA) documents in history, WikiLeaks released on Tuesday thousands of pages describing sophisticated software tools and techniques used by the agency to break into smartphones, computers and even Internet-connected televisions" (Shane, Rosenberg, Lehren). This was a disaster on many fronts. It was a disaster for the CIA and US intelligence operations, a failure for the concept of international diplomacy, and privacy for US citizens living aboard were skirted given the scope of the technological cyber tools discovered, democracy, and the US Government. The fallout was felt on March 7th, 2017, when the secret documents were released. Eventually, the source of the leak was captured, yet the damage was done. "Joshua Adam Schulte, who worked for a CIA group that designed computer code to spy on foreign adversaries, was believed to have provided the agency's top-secret information to WikiLeaks, federal prosecutors acknowledged in a hearing in January" (Harris). The first stage was called the Vault 7 documents, and it revealed a cyberweapon that made it confusing for forensic investigators to trace any evidence of a cyber-attack. For example, within the third part of the publication, "these anti-forensic tools allegedly used by the CIA in 2016 use obfuscation techniques to hide fragments of text in CIA-developed malware from detection. Obfuscators or packers are used to scramble the malware code making it difficult for both humans and programs to understand what it is, or attribute it to a specific source" (Mascarenhas). This reveal was particularly disrupting to cyber operations ran by the CIA against rogue states and international terrorist organizations and could have endangered critical assets in the field. On the other hand, questions exist on how much is left for Congressional oversight.

The publication of Vault 7 contained at least twenty-four parts describing the types of cyber operations employed by the CIA, and Vault 8 contained the corresponding code associated with the software. We will cover part four: Grasshopper; part five: Hive; part six: Weeping Angel, and part 11: Pandemic. To cover all parts would require more than one chapter; however, this is a case that will be continuously studied and analyzed to understand further the impact of the hack, and the implications of an intelligence agency in a democracy developing broad legal powers in cyberspace.

Part four was designed to "allow tools to be installed using a variety of persistence mechanisms and modified using a variety of extensions (like encryption). The requirements list of the

Automated Implant Branch (AIB) for Grasshopper puts special attention on PSP avoidance so that any *Personal Security Products* like 'MS Security Essentials,' 'Rising,' 'Symantac Endpoint' or 'Kaspersky IS' on target machines do not detect Grasshopper elements" (WikiLeaks). This was constructed as a systems manipulation tool that was "provided with a variety of modules that could be used by a CIA operator as blocks to construct a customized implant that will behave differently, for example maintaining persistence on the computer differently, depending on what particular features or capabilities are selected in the process of building the bundle" (WikiLeaks). This sort of software infrastructure would give the operator the capability to build malware designed to control and compromise Windows operation systems. For example, the blocks were utilized to construct and deconstruct known malware components (for data collection) like "Directinput Keylogger, Internet Explorer Password Collection, SetWindowsHookEx WH_KEYBOARD and WH_KEYBOARD_LL Key Logger, Webcam Capture, and Windows API Keyloggers"

(WikiLeaks). Of course, there was a limit found within the source code as "operators are able to build from very simple to very complex logic used to determine if a target device is running a specific version of Microsoft Windows, or if a particular Antivirus product is running or not" (WikiLeaks). This method was designed to check if the system was able to be penetrated without detection or penetrated at all as Grasshopper's limits were tested, then patched for continuous stealth capabilities. The source code for Grasshopper was not released in Vault 8.

Part five is a program called HIVE, designed as "a back-end infrastructure malware with a public-facing HTTPS interface which is used by CIA implants to transfer exfiltrated information from target machines to the CIA and to receive commands from its operators to execute specific tasks on the targets. The potential size and discretion of this malware makes it a powerful tool for cyberwarfare, and it can be "used across multiple malware implants and CIA operations. The public HTTPS interface utilizes unsuspicious looking cover domains to hide its presence"

(WikiLeaks). For example, it can be used in tracking targets internet use via financial transactions, peer-to-peer communications, or website use. Of course, if the target is sophisticated, the malware could be limited in gaining a clear pattern of use or location. Nonetheless, if a target has been infiltrated by intelligence, and a combination of intel on the ground and intel in cyberspace can organize a clear image from variable components, it makes a military strike not only possible, it can produce an accurate reprisal.

HIVE source code can be found on Wikileaks Vault 8 site repository. "The repository contains the following branches, 'armv5', 'autotools', 'debug', 'dhm', 'makemods', 'master', 'mt6', 'polar-0.14.3', 'polar-1.1.8', 'polar-1.2.11', 'polar-1.3.4', 'solarisbug' and 'ubiquiti'" (Wikileaks). There is also a downloadable zip file to get more code branches and revision information, yet you can find client, common, honeycomb, ilm-client, and server folder information within the repository.

Part six is the Weeping Angel malware on Vault 7, "an implant designed for Samsung F Series Smart Televisions. Based on the "Extending" tool from the MI5/BTSS, the implant is designed to record audio from the built-in microphone and egress or store the data" (Wikileaks). The Extending User Guide explains the malware in detail and gives a clear picture of its capabilities and its scope of operation. The mechanics are positioned out in a schematic that focuses on implementation. "The implant is configured in a Linux PC, and then deployed onto the TV using a USB stick. Audio files can then be extracted using a USB stick or setting up a Wi-Fi hotspot with-in range of the TV. It is also possible to listen to audio exfiltration live, using the Live Listen Tool, designed for use on a Windows OS" (Extending page. 2). Key features as also presented within the document enumerating first, "*Close Access Installation* is an EXTENDING implant to be installed using a *Close Access* method" (Extending, page 4). Second, "*Close Access Uninstall*, the EXTENDING implant can be uninstalled either by *Close Access* installation or at a pre-configured time" (Extending page. 4). Third, *"Close Access Audio File Retrieval* is the EXTENDING implant that can exfiltrate audio files to a USB stick" (Extending page. 4). Fourth, the *"Remote Audio File Retrieval* is the feature that exfiltrates audio files over a Wi-Fi hotspot" (Extending page. 4). Fifth, the *"Live Audio Listening* feature exfiltrates audio over a Wi-Fi hotspot to a *Live Listening Tool*, running on a laptop" (Extending page. 4). Lastly, the "Fake-off Recording will continue to record audio, even whilst the TV appears to be off" (Extending page. 4). These are the components of Weeping Angel malware that can be used to eavesdrop on targets in hotels, households, and public spaces towards a strategic political, economic, or military objectives.

Part Eleven in the Vault 7 release is the Pandemic malware, a "persistent implant for Microsoft Windows machines that share files (programs) with remote users in a local network. The application targets remote users by replacing application code on-the-fly with a trojaned version of the program retrieved from the infected machine" (WikiLeaks). Stealth is a crucial attribute for any segment of a counterintelligence apparatus, and Vault 7

reveals this aspect. "To obfuscate its activity, the original file on

the file server remains unchanged; it is only modified/replaced

while in transit from the pandemic file server before being

executed on the computer of the remote user" (WikiLeaks). This

application is applicable to local area network operations that

require information gathering within the target zone instead of

from a remote wide area network. For example, a cyber operation

that requires vital intelligence that is contained in a local server or

local data storage. This would require physical infiltration or an

internal asset within the target area for this method to be most

effective. Pandemic source code has not been released in Vault 8,

yet in the CIA Engineering Development Group Tool

Documentation release in Vault 7, technical specifications are laid

out, for example, 3.5 the installation and operations section states

"Pandemic will install via Shellterm's shellcode installer" (CIA

NSCG COL S-06), or the 3.4 configuration section that states

"Pandemic comes with a configuration utility (unclassified in 1.1)

which builds a binary file for execution via ShellTerm" (CIA NSCG

COL S-06). This document gives a general nominal view of the

technical scope of the malware, yet does not provide the source

code, most likely to keep it out of the wrong hands.

Given the information on these cyberweapons are public

knowledge, the controversy as to whether these programs threat

in and of themselves endanger the 4th Amendment protect

afforded by the US Bill of Rights if the government decides to turn

these applications in on citizens of the US, or the very nature of

the way these documents came into the public sphere violates US

law and endangers national security or the right to the freedom of

the press is all in the eye of the beholder. These points can be

argued and defended within chapters of their own as each issue is

complex and arduous. For the purpose of this publication, what is

being explored is the implications facing the oversight of the

power of these cyberweapons and who wields them, under

whose orders, and when. Can a presidency or the Congress

control the execution and the consequences of the use of such weapons in an effect to protect not only the national security of the republic, hitherto protect the cybersecurity of our critical infrastructure and assets? "The CIA, which is the US civilian foreign intelligence service, declined to comment on the authenticity of purported intelligence documents" (Walcott, Hosenball), and there is no visible record of Congressional oversight.

Consequently, it is currently unknown how this hack has impacted the government's ability to defend against its own cyberweaponry, and there is natural consequences indeed. "Cybersecurity experts have complained that the organization had possibly produced a technical blueprint on how to recreate the government's elite-level tools" (Stone). According to a Melbourne-based offensive security company Loop Secure, it has already been done, and this is one of the most devastating developments of the CIA hack. Cyberspace is an anarchic zone of cyberwarfare and spying, and if there is a lesson to learn from this case, it is the fact that cyberweapons are not solely own and used by nation-states, like nuclear, chemical, and biological weapons, and our international system has become even more dangerous than before.

References

Central Intelligence Agency: Information Operations Group. (2015). Engineering Development Group: Pandemic V1.1 Tool Documentation Rev. 1.1. *N/A Leaked Document,* 1-8. Retrieved May 18, 2019, from www.wikileaks.org.

Government Communication Headquarters. (2014). Extending User Guide. *N/A (Leaked Document),* 1-31. Retrieved from www.wikileaks.org. United Kingdom Government

Harris, S. (2018, May 15). US identifies suspect in major leak of CIA hacking tools. *Washington Post*. Retrieved from www.washingtonpost.com.world/national-security/us-ide...11e8-8836-a4a123c359ab_story.html?utm_term=.3adbfd99480b

Mascarenhas, H. (2017, April 01). WikiLeaks 'Marble' files: Latest leak exposes how CIA disguises its own hacking attacks. *International*

Business Times. Retrieved from www.ibtimes.co.uk/wikileaks-

marble-files-latest-leak-exposes-how-cia-disguises-its-own-

hacking-attacks-1614811

Shane, S., Rosenberg, M., & Lehren, A. (2017, March 07). WikiLeaks

Releases Trove of Alleged CIA Hacking Documents. *New York*

Times. Retrieved from

www.nytimes.com/2017/03/07/world/europe/wikileaks-cia-

hacking-html

Stone, J. (2019, February 27). A Researcher made an elite hacking

tool out of the info in the Vault 7 Leak. *Cyberscoop.* Retrieved

from www.cyberscoop.com/vault-7-operation-overwatch-cia-

hacking-tools-rsa-conference/

Walcott, J., & Hosenball, M. (2017, March 09). Source of the Lastest

WikiLeaks Document Dump Appears to Be CIA COntractors: US

Officals. *Time Magazine.* Retrieved from

www.time.com/4696405/wikileaks-cia-contractors-documents-

scource/

WikiLeaks. (n.d.). Vault 7: CIA Hacking Tools Revealed. Retrieved May

18, 2019, from www.wikileaks.org/ciav7p1/

WikiLeaks. (n.d.). Vault 8. Retrieved May 18, 2019, from

www.wikileaks.org/vault8

3

BAD RABBIT (ADOBE FLASH)

By: Jeff Falcon

The global cyberattacks that struck Ukrainian government agencies and international businesses during June 2017 served as a catalyst to invoke urgent discussions about how to identify and counter the latest made-to-order malware threats. This event served as another reminder for organizations to think critically about present and future state incident response processes, and to strategically manage cyber risks from the boardroom on down (Wired, 2017).

Leaders spanning both public and private sectors must remain focused on business and institutional risk and should understand that proactively blending and aligning resources to mitigate the likelihood of cybersecurity incidents will serve useful

in minimizing the damage when said attacks inevitably penetrate

defenses.

The Bad Rabbit Outbreak

Bad Rabbit first made its debut in October of 2017

targeting specific organizations in Russia and Ukraine along with

other regions in Eastern Europe. This attack was essentially an

industrial strength version of the NonPetya ransomware attack

that wreaked havoc earlier that year. Among the impacted

organizations were Kiev's metro system, Russian Media

organization Interfax and Odessa airport. "Interfax was forced to

publish to its Facebook page during the outage, since its servers

were taken offline for a number of hours" (The Guardian, 2019).

The Bad Rabbit malware encrypted data on infected machines

before demanding payment of XBT 0.05 (1/20th of a BitCoin),

valued approximately at $280 U.S. at the time of the attack. From

that point, the malware encrypted not only the target victim's

files, but also the systems' MBR (Master Boot Record). The

human-user was then promptly welcomed with a message on their screen asking them to submit payment via a Tor hidden service which was located on the Dark Web.

The Bad Rabbit outbreak initially appeared to have its roots tied to files that resided on compromised Russian media websites. Social engineering was leveraged to spread Bad Rabbit using watering hole attacks which eventually lead to the global spreading of a fake Adobe Flash installer. These compromised websites were used to deliver the fake Adobe Flash installer to website visitors from around the world. According to Ziyad Roumaya, Cybersecurity Practice Lead at CDW, "social engineering is the #1 avenue for hackers to exploit when targeting its victims. This method has been used since the beginning of time. It has now become the standard for targeting victims. The internet and social media has made it easier for hackers to gather information like this." (Roumaya, 2019). Once the bad guys have researched enough on the target through social engineering, they use the next easiest method to attack the target via ransomware. Most common ransomware would be delivered via email, but other

exploits can happen via vulnerabilities in applications, operating

systems or websites according to Roumaya. (Roumaya, 2019). An

example of these methods as previously pointed out; a watering

hole attack is a security exploit in which the attacker seeks to

compromise a specific group of end users by infecting websites

that members of the group are known to visit. The goal is to

infect a targeted user's computer and gain access to the network

at the target's place of employment. (Proofpoint, 2019).

Bad Rabbit Exploit Techniques

The Bad Rabbit outbreak used file naming conventions

mimicking the character names of the popular HBO series Game

of Thrones. Starting with rhaegal.job, this file was responsible for

executing the encryptor/decryptor upon the reboot of the system,

alongside drogon.job which was responsible for restarting the

victim's machine. A final file called viserion_23.job rebooted the target victim's machine a second time and would encrypt files within the system upon execution. Investigations produced further evidence that the Bad Rabbit outbreak used Microsoft SMB vulnerabilities patched in MS17-010, to propagate itself across a network. Bad Rabbit initially attempted to brute-force any administrative shares it found and would drop a copy of itself into these shares if this exploit was determined by it to be successful (path of least resistance). However, if the brute-force attack failed, then Bad Rabbit would resort to using an exploit focused on the previously mentioned vulnerabilities.

How does the SMB protocol work, and why was this so successful for the propagation of Bad Rabbit? The SMB protocol enables an application, or the user of an application to access files on a remote server, as well as, other resources including printers. Thus, a client application can open, read, move, create and update files on the remote server. It can also communicate with any server program that is setup to receive a SMB client request. The SMB protocol is known as a response-request protocol, meaning that it transmits multiple messages between the client and server to establish a connection (Varonis, 2019). Furthermore, upon leveraging the Microsoft SMB inherent protocol, the exploit was compounded due in part to the organization's failing to heed the recommended vulnerability and patch management guidance of the MS17-010 update bulletin. As described, Security update MS17-010 addresses several vulnerabilities in Windows Server Message Block (SMB) v1. The WannaCrypt ransomware is exploiting one of the vulnerabilities that is part of the MS17-010 update. Computers that do not have MS17-010 installed are at heightened risk because of several strains of malware (Microsoft Support, 2019).

Pragmatic Preventative Measures

Cybercriminals very often take advantage of known exploits; however, it is important to keep in mind that many vendors also routinely publish patches for organizations and their users which in turn can help protect themselves adequately from attacks. In addition to tactical prevention practices, such as habitually backing up files, instilling education on the impacts of ransomware and incorporating multi-layered security solutions and strategies, the following guidelines should be considered at a strategic level as well (Sophos, 2019).

Instill strong security hygiene to help with the prevention of ransomware from entering your environment through commonly attacked vectors such as email and network perimeter gateways. In conjunction with assuring that end user accounts are locked down from their client administrator privileges, a strong basic hygiene stance will drastically reduce nefarious software installs that may be downloaded from website activity.

Additionally, it is also imperative to implement and rehearse incident response planning and crisis management exercises. These activities will help establish or mature the formal procedures which govern the flow of accountability and incorporate the stakeholders that are critical in making key decisions in the heat of the moment.

Disciplined routines that incorporate patch and vulnerability management are paramount to building out a robust response plan. The tools and processes associated with these activities will help reduce the overall likelihood of exploitation and will help ensure that the victim organization is able to respond and recover from the impact of an attack.

References:

Bad Rabbit: Game of Thrones-referencing ransomware hits

Europe. The Guardian, 2019

https://www.theguardian.com/technology/2017/oct/25/bad-rabbit-game-of-thrones-ransomware-europe-notpetya-bitcoin-decryption-key

How to verify that MS17-010 is installed. Microsoft Support

Publication, 2019.

https://support.microsoft.com/en-us/help/4023262/how-to-verify-that-ms17-010-is-installed

Roumaya, Ziyad. Cybersecurity Practice Lead, CDW. Personal Communication 2019.

Sophos, Naked Security. 2018.

https://nakedsecurity.sophos.com/tag/bad-rabbit/

The Bad Rabbit malware was disguised as a Flash update.

Wired UK, (Matt Burgess), Friday October 27, 2017.

https://www.wired.co.uk/article/bad-rabbit-ransomware-flash-explained

What is a watering hole attack? Proofpoint Threat Publication, 2019. https://www.proofpoint.com/us/threat-reference/watering-hole

What is an SMB Port + Ports 445 and 139 explained. Varonis Blog. January 4, 2019.

https://www.varonis.com/blog/smb-port/

4

HBO

By: Lyda Tesauro

On July 31, 2017, almost three years after the infamous

Sony Pictures hack, the entertainment industry suffered another

major blow. On that fateful day and within the following weeks,

news broke that hackers infiltrated HBO's networks, accessed

HBO's key network infrastructure, stole a total of 1.5 terabytes of

data, illegally procured thousands of HBO internal documents,

published an abundance of copyrighted items (e.g., documents,

images, video, and sound), released unaired episodes of certain

TV series (e.g., "Ballers," "Insecure," "Room 104," an unreleased

show at the time called "Barry," "Curb Your Enthusiasm," and

"The Deuce"), posted the script of an unaired fourth episode of the seventh season of Game of Thrones, leaked the personal

information of a senior HBO executive via a text document,

compromised the online accounts of the same senior HBO

executive (e.g., the paid newspaper subscriptions, the online

banking, and the personal health services), and published

screenshots of HBO's internal administration tools (e.g., listing

employee names, email addresses, and functions within the

organization) (Roettger, 2017; Rindner, 2017). Additionally, the

hackers also accessed HBO's internal corporate email/email

servers, the personal information of their customers, and the

customers' account; however, the damage in this particular area

was limited (Roettger, 2017). Although this was a terrible

situation and a complete publicity nightmare for HBO, the cable

company was lucky to have the FBI and Mandiant's help during

that difficult time (Ridner, 2017). Based on the severity of this

cyberattack, it is safe to say that HBO was not prepared for the

coming winter (a potential breach) and should have taken the

House of Stark's motto a little more seriously. In order to help readers fully understand the severity of this hack, I will analyze how the crime occurred, discuss how the incidents could have been avoided, delve into the ramifications of the breach, and mention some of the lessons HBO as well as the entertainment industry can learn from this unfortunate event.

How the Incidents Occurred and Could Have Been Avoided

When the news initially went viral, many experts in the field started speculating how the cyber incidents occurred and started making statements that the HBO hackers were in HBO's systems for months prior to the public's knowledge (Nelson, 2017). According to their earlier reports, the experts believed that either the hackers were able to gain unauthorized access to HBO's networks by targeting HBO employees and exploiting their human errors, or they were able to gain unauthorized access because HBO utilized old technology (particularly older versions of Windows) to house its content (Nelson, 2017). Unfortunately, reports confirming or denying those theories were not made known to the public until several days after the incident was first

mentioned.

Eventually, in the middle of August, the public was informed

that there were, in fact, four distinct cyber incidents that made up

the HBO hack (Barrett, 2017). Based on the most recent findings,

the incidents stemmed from a lack of adequate network

protection (both from a human and technological perspective),

supply chain issues, malicious insiders, accidental insiders, and

account compromise—all of which could have been avoided if the

proper cyber practices were followed (Barrett, 2017).

According to reports regarding the first incident, hackers

identified only as Mr. Smith released four unaired episodes of

HBO shows and garnered 1.5 terabytes of HBO's data (Barrett,

2017). In the words of the hacker or hacking group, four key

pieces of information were exposed: a) that this cyber attack was

a six month effort, b) that they were able to bypass network

protections through holes unknown to both the public and

technology companies by utilizing zero-day exploits, c) that they not only wanted anonymous fame but also monetary gain (since

the hacker or hacking group wanted $7 million in ransom in

exchange for an end to the information leaks), and d) that they

most likely had the access that they claimed after they posted

screenshots of HBO's file directory as well as important

documents in waves in an attempt to bully HBO into paying the

ransom (Barrett, 2017; Dark Owl, 2017). Even though HBO

probably wanted the hacks and leaks to stop, they ultimately

made the right decision and did not pay the ransom—despite

conversing with the hackers or hacking group (Dark Owl, 2017).

Although this incident alone would have been huge, more

attacks followed—which is not uncommon. This time, a full

episode of *Game of Thrones* was leaked two days early by four

Indian men (Barrett, 2017). According to reports, three Prime

Focus Technologies' employees and one former employee were

able to access the episode and, for whatever reason, released the

episode online without authorization (Barrett, 2017). They were

able to do this because Prime Focus Technologies works with Star

India, which carries HBO in that country, and has access to Start India accounts (Barrett, 2017). Because numerous people are involved in the making and distribution of digital entertainment, supply chain and malicious insider threats are becoming more of a problem for the entertainment industry—especially since more people are given access to a particular work product, therefore, the chances of something going wrong dramatically increases.

As if these incidents were not enough, HBO Nordic and HBO España accidentally aired an episode an hour ahead of schedule due to an error from a third-party vendor (Barrett, 2017). Although the episode was removed as soon the mistake was caught, multiple individuals illegally posted the episode on torrent sites so HBO did face some repercussions from this unfortunate turn of events (Barrett, 2017).

Finally, the last known cyber incident HBO faced in 2017 was the OurMine hack (Barrett, 2017). According to reports, the hacking group (OurMine) took over HBO's social media accounts and informed the company that they needed to update their security (Barrett, 2017). Although the account compromise damage was minute, it was still another embarrassing ordeal that HBO had to endure.

In closing, I will admit that HBO and all large corporations do face multiple challenges when it comes to effectively protecting their networks; however, at some point HBO needed to have stepped up its cyber and information security game. Since HBO was aware of the fact that the entertainment industry's cyber and information security practices were five to six years behind overall industry norms, they were aware of the ramifications of the Sony hack, and they were aware of the fact that their cyber practices needed to have been improved (because they had already been hacked prior to this most recent cyber incident), a hack of this nature never should have happened to them if they had implemented a better cybersecurity and information security program within their organization (Dark Owl, 2017; Nelson, 2017).

What Were the Ramifications

Naturally, as with any data breach, there were some investigative (e.g., forensic), legal, reputational, and security (e.g., physical, cyber, and information security) costs that did put a burden on HBO. After the hack became public, HBO was swiftly labeled vulnerable by many hackers in the cyber realm, which essentially put a target on the company's back (Spangler, 2017). Although HBO had its fair share of misfortunes after the initial incident, HBO was surprisingly able to recover from an incident of this caliber better than any other entertainment company in the industry to date—which is honestly a miracle. Aside from the aforementioned string of cyber attacks, leaks, and nuisances listed in the previous section, HBO only faced slight financial and reputational ramifications in comparison to Sony Pictures (Barrett, 2017). In fact, HBO somehow managed to still maintain viewership and gain public sympathy over the ordeal, despite the fact that other companies had tried and failed in the past to invoke pity in its customer base. Furthermore, in the midst of the drama and embarrassment caused by HBO's very public cyber incidents, AT&T continued with the business plan to acquire Time Warner, HBO's parent company—even though the company was under physical and judgmental attacks at the time (Barrett, 2017). In order to reduce the threat landscape and limit the severity of cyber ramifications, HBO needs to learn from its mistakes and implement better cybersecurity as well as information security practices.

What Are the Lessons Learned

Although HBO executives probably want the 2017 hack to disappear altogether, there are some lessons that need to be learned from this situation and things that need to be rectified. In my opinion, the main lesson that should be learned from this hack is that the entertainment industry has its work cut out for them when it comes to revamping their cyber and information security programs. Essentially, HBO needs to create as well as implement SATPs in order to reduce human error, buy good technology that will help secure multiple points of entry, implement a password management program, utilize a two-factor authentication for social media accounts, and initiate a patching program.

Hopefully, the HBO leaders will learn from their mistakes and will

strive to mitigate cyber incidents before they get out of hand.

Conclusion

Throughout this paper, I addressed the HBO hack, analyzed

how the incidents occurred, discussed how the data breaches

could have been avoided, delved into the ramifications of the data

breach, and mentioned some of the lessons HBO—as well as

other information security lax companies—could have learned

from this tragedy. In conclusion, I sincerely hope that this paper

enlightens people—especially people in the entertainment

industry—on the importance of information security and its

proper practices so that both cyber attacks and hacks of this

nature are reduced.

References

Barrett, B. (2017, August 18). Breaking Down HBO's Brutal Month

of Hacks. Retrieved from

https://www.wired.com/story/hbo-hacks-game-of-thrones/

Dark Owl (2017, August 18). An in-depth explanation of the recent

the HBO hacks. Retrieved from

https://www.darkowl.com/blog/2017/hbo-hacks-explained-

in-depth

Nelson, K. (2017, August 07). How the HBO Hack Happened,

According to an Expert. Retrieved from

https://www.digitaltrends.com/movies/hbo-hack-explained/

Rindner, G. (2017, August 07). The HBO hack: What we know (and

what we don't). Retrieved from

https://www.vox.com/2017/8/5/16095560/hbo-hack-details-

game-of-thrones

Roettgers, J. (2017, August 02). HBO Security Contractor: Hackers

Stole 'Thousands of Internal Documents' (EXCLUSIVE).

Retrieved from https://variety.com/2017/digital/news/hbo-

hack-thousands-of-documents-stolen-1202513573/

Spangler, T. (2017, August 18). HBO Hacks and Leaks: How Much

Have They Hurt the Business? Retrieved from

https://variety.com/2017/digital/news/hbo-hacks-leaks-

business-impact-1202531385/

5

NICE HASH

By: Charles Young

Cryptocurrency is a recent phenomenon which has captured the imagination of many investors, technologists, futurists, and enthusiasts. The term "cryptocurrency" was first used in 1990 as a descriptive noun combining "crypto" and "currency" to describe "any form of currency that only exists digitally, that usually has no central issuing or regulating authority but instead uses a decentralized system to record transactions and manage the issuance of new units, and that relies on cryptography to prevent counterfeiting and fraudulent transactions" (Merriam-Webster, 2018).

Even though the term cryptocurrency was first used almost 30 years ago, actual cryptocurrency has only recently become a reality. On January 3, 2009, a programmer under the pseudonym, Satoshi Nakamoto, invented Bitcoin (Davis, 2011). Previous attempts to design cryptocurrency could not sufficiently prevent a user from using a unit of digital currency twice without a third party ledger. Nakamoto suggested using a peer-to-peer network to solve the "double-spending problem", thus creating the "world's first completely decentralized digital-payments system" (Brito & Castillo, 2013). Bitcoin's decentralization coupled with anonymous usage has contributed to its ever increasing popularity.

As the popularity of Bitcoin has increased, other similar cryptocurrencies have been created along with associated services to make all types of cryptocurrency more accessible and less costly to the average person. Once such service is Slovenian based NiceHash, which serves as an intermediary marketplace to allow users to buy and sell computing power which is required in order to generate or "mine" cryptocurrency. NiceHash was created in 2014 and claims to be the "world's largest crypto-mining marketplace with over 293,000 buyers and over 108,000 miners (NiceHash, 2017).

On December 7, 2017, a post from NiceHash on the social website, Reddit, read, "Unfortunately, there has been a security breach involving NiceHash website. We are currently investigating the nature of the incident and, as a result, we are stopping all operations for the next 24 hours. Importantly, our payment system was compromised and the contents of the NiceHash Bitcoin wallet have been stolen. We are working to verify the precise number of [BitCoin] BTC taken" (NiceHash, 2017). NiceHash ordered users to change their passwords as a precaution and stated that the authorities had been notified. Additionally, NiceHash notified major BitCoin exchanges and sites in an effort to increase awareness and possibly prevent coin usage.

In the following days, details about the attack began to emerge as NiceHash began attempting to curb public anxiety. Marko Kobal, one of the cofounders and NiceHash CEO, stated, "Yesterday morning at about 1 a.m. a hacker or a group of hackers was able to infiltrate our systems through a compromised company computer," (Iyengar, 2017). NiceHash head of marketing, Andrej P. Škraba, explained that the hack was "a highly professional attack with sophisticated social engineering," (Reuters, 2017). Additional information from NiceHash clarified that a hacker using an IP address outside the European Union compromised a company computer, stole an engineer's credentials, and infiltrated NiceHash's internal network to steal funds from user accounts. In an appearance on Facebook Live, Kobal stated that "forensic analysis" involving local and international authorities was taking place, but did not expand on which specific agencies were involved when asked by the BBC (Lee, 2017). Website CoinGecko co-founder Brian Ong and many cryptocurrency users are speculated that "...it could be an inside job or a phishing attack on one of the employees" (Akhtar, 2017). NiceHash and Kobal continued to state that the attack was "incredibly coordinated" but clearly the company had a major hole in its security (Kan, 2018). The specific details of what happened have never been released, but it is clear the social component of the hack played an integral part in its success.

NiceHash was back online within two weeks after the attack and the company promised to fully reimburse losses of all users. During the relaunch, it was announced that Kobal had been replaced and had sold his 45% stake in the company (Peterson, 2017). A new security measure had been implemented in the NiceHash marketplace payment system which required the manual confirmation of every cryptocurrency transaction that leaves its systems (Kan, 2018).

In the initial press release describing the incident, NiceHash did not indicate how much BitCoin had been stolen from its wallet (a digital repository of "coins"). According to some NiceHash users, a BitCoin wallet address belonging to the anonymous attacker suggests that 4,736 BitCoin were stolen which, at the time, equated to approximately $62 million (Higgins, 2017). The company has promised to pay back its users and as of April 1, 2019, 74% of the stolen funds have been reimbursed. NiceHash continues to pay out reimbursements in periodic 1% increments (NiceHash, 2019).

According to Patrick McCorry, research associate at the University College London and the UK's first PhD graduate in cryptocurrencies, BitCoin thefts are unique in that once they are stolen, they become property of the thief. Fortunately, if the stolen coins are made public it would make it very difficult for hackers to actually use or convert the coins. (Akhtar, 2017). Unfortunately, it does not appear that the stolen coins have been made public.

Cryptocurrency has been touted as a safe, secure alternative to traditional currency. Unfortunately, every time a hack occurs, fears that cryptocurrency cannot be a viable replacement for traditional currency arise. In the case of BitCoin, "Bitcoin owners can spend, sell, trade, donate or otherwise use their bitcoins with little fear of the strong cryptography behind it being cracked. It's as close to bulletproof as you'll get – so long as you keep your private keys private" (Armerding, 2017) referring to exchange sites which require private keys to make BitCoin trading easier. By transferring private keys, the user is beholden to the intermediary site's security. This is an important distinction which further amplifies the issue with the NiceHash hack was due to the intermediary, not the cryptocurrency. However, casual observers may not see this distinction.

It is hard to see cryptocurrency gaining widespread acceptance like a traditional currency in the near future. Incidents like the NiceHash hack do not help with public opinion. Even though the hack was of the intermediary and not the cryptocurrency itself, the negative publicity garnered reflected more on the volatility of Bitcoin and not poor security practices of NiceHash.

References

Akhtar, A. (2017, December 8). The $70 Million Bitcoin Hack Was

the 4th Largest Breach in Cryptocurrency History. Retrieved

from http://money.com/money/5056652/the-70-million-

bitcoin-hack-was-the-4th-largest-breach-in-cryptocurrency-

history/

Armerding, T. (2017, October 2). Bitcoin's soft and vulnerable

underbelly. Retrieved from

https://nakedsecurity.sophos.com/2017/10/02/bitcoins-soft-

and-vulnerable-underbelly/

Brito, J., & Castillo, A. (2013). Bitcoin: A Primes for Policymakers.

Arlington: Mercatus Center at George Mason University.

Crypomaniaks. (2018, October 9). Do You Know the 5 Different

Types of Cryptocurrency? | Medium. Retrieved from

https://medium.com/predict/do-you-know-the-5-different-

types-of-cryptocurrency-medium-29298d1fad2f

Davis, J. (2011, October 3). The Crypto-Currency: Bitcoin and its mysterious inventor. Retrieved from

www.newyorker.com/magazine/2011/10/10/the-crypto-

currency

Higgins, S. (2017, December 7). Cryptocurrency Mining Market

NiceHash Hacked. Retrieved from

https://www.coindesk.com/62-million-gone-cryptocurrency-

mining-market-nicehash-hacked

Iyengar, R. (2017, December 8). More than $70 million stolen in

bitcoin hack. Retrieved from

https://money.cnn.com/2017/12/07/technology/nicehash-

bitcoin-theft-hacking/index.html

Kan, M. (2018, June 22). 7 Huge Hacks That Might Make You Think

Twice About Cryptocurrency. Retrieved from

https://www.pcmag.com/news/362000/crypto-exchange-

hacks

Lee, D. (2017, December 8). Millions 'stolen' in NiceHash Bitcoin

heist. Retrieved from

https://www.bbc.com/news/technology-42275523

Merriam-Webster. (2018, May 13). cryptocurrency. Retrieved

from https://www.merriam-

webster.com/dictionary/cryptocurrency

Nakamoto, S. (2017, May 14). Bitcoin: A Peer-to-Peer Electronic

Cash System. Retrieved from https://bitcoin.org/bitcoin.pdf

NiceHash. (2017, December 7). Reddit. Retrieved from

https://www.reddit.com/r/NiceHash/comments/7i0s6o/offici

al_press_release_statement_by_nicehash/

NiceHash. (2019, March 29). Fifteenth reimbursement of the

Repayment program. Retrieved from

https://www.nicehash.com/news/fifteenth-reimbursement-

of-the-repayment-program

Peterson, B. (2017, December 29). Bitcoin startup NiceHash has a

new CEO just weeks after hackers stole $63 million form the

company. Retrieved from

https://www.businessinsider.com/bitcoin-startup-nicehash-

replaced-its-ceo-soon-after-63-million-hack-2017-12

6

DEEPROOTS

By: Jeff Mendenhall

It can be said that any organizational possessing the data of millions upon millions of individuals, should be required to maintain adequate and efficient security controls. Current privacy and data laws within the United States of America do not necessarily protect every aspect of personal data or even personally identifiable information. The information lost in the Deep Roots Analytics Incident is not necessarily critical personal data, but the data can be damaging to individuals whose data was lost. The information involved in the information security breach contained the home addresses, birthdays, phone numbers and other general data. The information by itself is not particularly damaging, but the aggregated personal data is damaging. "The

Deep Root server — which was publicly accessible between June 1

and June 12 — included data collected by other firms and

Republican super PACs, including voters' home addresses,

birthdates, phone numbers and opinions on political issues"

(Reilly, 2017). The overall disregard for protecting personal data

controlled by the massive data firms, Internet search engines, and

social media platforms is astonishing. Currently, the only legal

impact facing the firm Deep Root Analytics is a public

embarrassment, ridicule and most likely numerous civil lawsuits.

The enormous volumes of data obtained by the various

organizations involved within the Republican National Committee

(RNC) 2016 are participants in the Deep Root Analytics

information security breach. An important fact to remember

concerning the Deep Root Analytics breach, is that numerous

organizations collected the data. There were multiple data

analysis firms involved in collecting personal data on American

voters. Cambridge Analytica was another firm involved in

collecting personal data. Cambridge Analytica presumably

violated Facebook's data access policies with the inappropriate

scanning of Facebook user profiles. Cambridge Analytica then

aggregated the Facebook user data with other firms involved in

collecting data for the Republican National Committee or RNC.

"Many of the files did not originate at Deep Root but are instead

the aggregate of outside data firms and Republican super PACs,

shedding light onto the increasingly advanced data ecosystem

that helped propel President Donald Trump's slim margins in key

swing states" (Cameron, Conger, 2018). It is just another firm

erroneously and irresponsibly obtaining personal voter data.

"Cambridge Analytica, a political data firm hired by President

Trump's 2016 election campaign, gained access to private

information on more than 50 million Facebook users. The firm

offered tools that could identify the personalities of American

voters and influence their behavior" (Granville, 2018). The

information security breach involving Deep Root Analytics firm is

not the only secure gathering data on individuals, organizations, and groups. It is an individual, group or organization wanting to obtain any relevant or irrelevant data on individuals. The problem with irrelevant data is that once irrelevant is aggregated, it has the potential to be extremely relevant data with potential impact.

The primary cause of the Deep Root Analytics breach was with internal organizational controls. In the information provided through various reference articles in numerous news reports, the data involved in the information security breach was left exposed on a server hosted by Amazon cloud services. An information security analyst employed by "UpGuard Incorporated" an information security firm. "UpGuard cyber risk analyst Chris Vickery discovered Deep Root's data online last week. More than a terabyte were stored on the cloud server without the protection of a password and could be accessed by anyone who found the URL" (Cameron, Conger, 2018). The most elementary information security principles were not followed, attempted or even remotely considered by the individuals within these organizations. The primary issue was transferring the aggregated data to an unsecured cloud-based server. The cloud-based server was serviced through Amazon. However, it does not appear that Deep Root Analytics purchased any additional services in the form of security, and only purchased cloud-based storage. It is also necessary to point out, it was up to Deep Root Analytics to secure the cloud-based storage or at the very least pay for information security services. As with any cloud-based service, you pay for each service from storage space, access controls to information security services. The most incredible aspect concerning the issues with Deep Root Analytics data management processes is change control. One of the basic concepts within any organizations information technology policies and procedures is change control. Change control processes allows an organizations information technology teams to discuss and concur on any upgrades or service interruptions. These processes should be clearly described in any basic information technology and security policies. "The data was exposed following a software upgrade, when the company forgot to turn on the password protection again" (Rash, 2017). A simple change control process should have caught the configuration error after the change was completed.

You do not have to be an information security professional to understand the basics of information security, even the data analysts working for Deep Root Analytics and Cambridge Analytics should have a basic understanding of information security principles and concepts. The unsecured data was quickly located by an information security analyst and reported accordingly. The numerous nefarious individuals mining for data on the Internet makes even the most non-technical only wonder who accessed the unsecured data. How long was it available, who downloaded the data, and for what purposes.

The ramifications involving the Deep Root Analytics incident and the aggregated data from several data analytic firms are still developing. There will be numerous civil actions and lawsuits involving the data analytic firms associated with Deep Root Analytics breach. It is unknown on what the exact level of damage to individuals whose data was lost through gross

misconduct by the various data analytic firms. However, a current

class action lawsuit against Deep Root Analytics has already been

filed. "direct and proximate cause of Deep Root's conduct," those

exposed in the data breach may be vulnerable to identity theft

and "a loss of privacy," and argue that the "actual damages"

exceed $5 million" (Bertrand, 2017). The damage to the analytical

firms will be monetary in the form of lawsuits, settlements and

bankruptcy proceedings. The impact to individuals whose data

was lost through gross negligence will be exceptional and ongoing

for decades. The aggregated personal data lost to the Internet is

unrecoverable, as once data enters the Internet, it will remain on

the Internet. The information for a specific John Doe will be

readily available for anyone attempting to damage the individual

directly or indirectly through massive fraud activities.

Hopefully, the business sector involving data analytics will

have learned from the Deep Root Analytics information security

breach. It would be interesting to understand the extent of any information technology and security policies and procedures existing within the Deep Root Analytics firm. In reviewing the aspects of this particular information security incident, it would appear that the organizations lacked a basic information security policy and therefore lacked the associated procedures. The massive level of incompetence and lack of interest in securing the incredible volume of data involving almost two-thirds of registered voters in the United States is amazing. At the very least, the data should have been password protected and access controls involving the various organizations accessing the data. The numerous articles and presentations involving the security breach fail to mention how long the data was unsecured on the Internet. As an information security professional, it would be interesting to obtain the length of time the data was exposed and how many times it was accessed and downloaded. Unfortunately, that information will be impossible to obtain, before the beginning of any civil actions or individual lawsuits against the various data analytical firms involved.

The basic protections of personal data in the form of personally identifiable information (PII) in the United States are inadequate. We currently have no current or pending Federal laws to protect personally identifiable information. The European Union has numerous laws protecting individuals from various forms of data mining involving individuals, organizations and the most significant technical organizations in the world. It is time for the United States to move to protect the ownership of personal data and prevent further monetary gain and misuse from the social media and technical giants. An individual should be able to own their personal data and determine who or what is allowed access to it. At the very least, individuals should be reimbursed by technical and analytical firms for any monetary gains obtained through distribution of study of personal data. The individual should have complete ownership of their personal information and it uses.

References

Bertrand, N. (2017, June 22). GOP data firm that exposed millions of Americans' personal information is facing its first class-action lawsuit. Retrieved from http://www.businessinsider.com/deep-root-analytics-sued-after-data-breach-2017-6

Granville, K. (2018, March 19). Facebook and Cambridge Analytica: What You Need to Know as Fallout Widens. Retrieved from https://www.nytimes.com/2018/03/19/technology/facebook -cambridge-analytica-explained.html

O'Hara, R. (2018, April 03). What Facebook knows about me | Rosemary O'Hara. Retrieved from http://www.sun-sentinel.com/opinion/fl-op-column-what-facebook-knows-rosemary-ohara-20180403-story.html

Rash, W. (2018, May 18). Astonishing Level of Ineptitude Exposed in RNC Breach. Retrieved from http://www.eweek.com/security/astonishing-level-of-ineptitude-exposed-in-rnc-breac

Reilly, K. (2017, June 20). Nearly 200 Million U.S. Voters' Personal Data Accidentally Leaked. Retrieved from http://fortune.com/2017/06/19/deep-root-analytics-voter-data-exposed/

UpGuard Inc. [Cyber Security Business]. (2018, May 10).

7

VERIZON / NICE SYSTEMS

By: William "Cody" Harris

The immense growth of the technology industry has put an alarming amount of consumer data in the hands of companies. For most people, they are willing to accept the fact that a company that they have knowingly and intentionally engaged with, holds this information, and they trust that this company will do what is necessary to protect their private or sensitive information. From social media accounts and internet service providers, to insurance companies or even waste service, companies often hold a consumer's name, phone number, address, and payment information in the form of bank account and/or credit card information. In this age of fast-paced convenience, this is an acceptable or even necessary risk for most consumers. What many do not realize, however, is that their information is likely in the hands of far more entities than just the ones they know about, and therefore exposed to exponentially more risk than otherwise believed.

Third-party data management and service providers have become an attractive option for companies large and small for many reasons. By in large their popularity has grown because of the services they offer to help manage the inordinate amount of customer data that a primary company may acquire. The unique data processing capabilities that third-party vendors specialize in, allows the primary company to offload the costs of developing and operating their own data management systems to get even better results from a specialized third-party vendor. Unfortunately, many of these third-party vendors are not held to the same information security standards and in the case of foreign entities, many do not have to meet the same federal requirements for data security practices as primary U.S. based companies. What makes this situation even more dangerous is that in some cases their data security and risk management practices are not even evaluated by the primary company. In fact, a recent survey of over 1000 Chief

Information Security Officers (CISO) from the U.S. and U.K.

conducted by the Ponemon Institute, found that companies on

average share sensitive data with 583 third-parties, and that up to

61% of the CISOs surveyed, said that they have suffered a data

breach caused by third-party vendors. Alarmingly, 57% of these

individuals claimed that they were unsure if their company's third-

party vendors implemented safeguards that were effective in

preventing data breaches (Kelly, 2018). The market for third-party

data management services is ripe, which means that the number of

potentially poorly secured companies is growing as well. Without

the intervention of the primary company to ensure that data

security and risk management practices are sufficent, this translates

to increased consumer risk.

In June of 2017, this third-party risk came to fruition for

Verizon and as many as 6 million of their customers. An Israeli

based third-party vendor by the name of NICE Systems, who

Verizon uses for a portion of their back-office and call center

operations, allowed one of their Amazon Web Services (AWS)

Simple Storage Service (S3) cloud storage buckets to be publicly

accessible. The information contained within this cloud storage bucket included customer data in the form of names, addresses, phone numbers, PIN codes, as well as customer service call transcripts. It wasn't until the Director of Cyber Risk Research, Chris Vickery of UpGuard, an independent cybersecurity and third-party risk management company, notified Verizon of the publicly accessible and fully downloadable data on June 13th, 2017, that action was taken to secure the breach. By June 22nd, Verizon and NICE Systems had corrected the S3 misconfiguration that led to the exposed data (O'Sullivan, 2018).

Further analysis of the breach uncovered an even more disturbing reality than the already disconcerting exposure millions of customer's sensitive data to the world-wide-web, however. Evaluation of the data stored on the NICE Systems S3 bucket revealed a collection and log of customer call information which was being composed for unknown purposes and without the knowledge or direction of Verizon. What makes this even more concerning is the NICE Systems' links to state-sponsored development of intrusive surveillance technology in countries where privacy laws are lax at best (Frenkel, 2015). This information gives rise to the serious concerns that American companies like Verizon, may be inadvertently providing foreign entities with a considerable amount of data on American citizens. While this has not been confirmed to be the intent behind NICE Systems collection of Verizon customer's information, it is easily a deeply concerning possibility.

So, what is the danger of such an exposure?

Well aside from the obvious sensitive and personal information that was exposed, this breach allowed the potential for someone to circumvent the two-factor authentication process, allowing unadulterated access to a customer's Verizon account. With such access it is possible for someone to conduct sim-swap scams or even hijack calls and messages of that user, effectively enabling full-time surveillance of their regular communication (O'Sullivan, 2018). With Verizon possessing the largest market share of wireless business in the U.S., at more than 151 million subscribers, the potential for this type of information to be used as leverage for a nefarious actor to blackmail a high valued individual, is quite possible (Holst, 2019). The introduction of potentially foreign state-sponsored involvement in this situation is where the issues with this event certainly become exponentially more troubling. With the deep pockets of a state government to provide significant resources, manpower, and money, with this type of exposed information in hand, it could be possible to mount an effort to gain surveillance access to some of the most important people in the country.

So, who is to blame?

In cyber breach events such as this one, the blame isn't always so easily identified. With multiple entities involved and various levels of the use and possession of this customer information, the blame is often shared. It could be easy to point at Verizon being to blame for not ensuring that their third-party vendors were conducting proper cybersecurity practices and not properly vetting that vendor's operational procedures with their customer information. Not to mention, the use of this vendor could have potentially exposed U.S. citizens to nefarious state-sponsored actors.

In other cases, some might point the finger at Amazon and their seemingly easily misconfigured S3 services. After all, this isn't the first major exposure of customer information due to the misconfiguration of S3 services. Just a few short weeks after the Verizon incident, a similar issue revealed the personal information of three million World Wrestling Entertainment fans and another misconfigured S3 bucket exposed nearly 198 million American's information being held by an organization working for the Republican National Committee (Newman, 2017 & O'Sullivan, 2019). While directly blaming Amazon for a users misconfiguration of their services is quite a stretch, providing built-in security features to protect against common misconfigurations is certainly the more cybersecurity conscious thing to do. In light of this event, and many like it, Amazon has since addressed the common misconfigurations of public-facing

S3 buckets by introducing a "Public Access Settings For This Account" feature on the S3 dashboard. This feature automatically applies to all new and existing S3 buckets within a single account, automatically overriding existing Access Control Lists (ACL) and policies. This prevents the user from having to access each and every S3 bucket to have to make these changes manually, and therefore potentially misconfiguring them (Cimpanu, 2018).

While there is plenty of blame to go around, NICE Systems is undoubtedly at the greatest fault for being the ones who directly made the error that allowed the breach possibility. It doesn't take much examination to identify where NICE went wrong in this event. Poor security configuration practices combined with the questionable practice of storing call log and customer information without the knowledge or direction of Verizon or their customers, certainly puts a significant burden of guilt on NICE Systems in the end.

So, where does the responsibility of cybersecurity end for an enterprise?

In cases such as this, where does the responsibility to protect consumer data end for a company like Verizon? Should we as consumers be comfortable that large corporations that have access to our personal data conduct effective cybersecurity operations themselves, but leave their third-party vendors (who by connection, also have access to our data) to their own cybersecurity practices with no corporate oversight? Obviously, there is a level of responsibility that is required of corporations and much of that is governed by a growing number of state and national legislations. In fact, just this year more than 260 bills and resolutions were introduced by 45 different states and Puerto Rico that addressed cybersecurity related concerns, however, like with any government established levels of protection, there are limitations by way of resource availability and therefore enforceability (Cybersecurity Legislation 2019, 2019). The other challenge that is posed to such pieces of legislation is the task of writing a law that is comprehensive yet not oppressive. The fine line between allowing a company to conduct a secure and profitable business, versus regulating them so much that they choose to relocate their business where these rules and regulations are not as severe. Companies definitely have a responsibility to protect their customer's information, but in reality, a consumer will only ever be as secure as they are knowledgeable. Consumers should take it upon themselves to conduct their own due diligence and research how the companies they deal with handle cybersecurity and what that company's history of data breaches looks like.

So, what is the solution?

Best practices for third party vendors have certainly improved in recent years, in part due to the increased number of exposed events like that of the Verizon incident. Continued breaches have shed new light on avenues of exposure for companies large and small. With the current rate of consumer data generation showing no signs of slowing, it is essential that companies find better ways of securely managing this data. One of the best places to start is with some of the pre-established security frameworks that are available. Security frameworks, such as PCI DSS, ISO 27001/27002, and NIST Frameworks, offer proven methods of evaluating a company's current information security practices and policies, as well as ways to implement new ones. This effectively establishes a secure foundation from which companies can continue to build more secure business operations, often reveling areas that would have otherwise gone unnoticed and therefore insecure. In many cases, companies may even choose to adopt a hybrid approach to the offered security frameworks in order to tailor a program that best suits their business needs and the needs of their customers (Moraetes, 2018).

Adopting a security framework is a great place to start for most companies, but that cannot be the only thing that the organization does to protect its data. When the question, "How do you address the issue of third-party vendor risk?" was posed to a panel of CISOs at the 2019 Norwich University Cyber Security Summit, the responses addressed various, but complementary solutions. One response from Lumber Liquidators CISO, Tyson Martin, was to adopt a risk-tiered approach. In this approach, the company would evaluate the information that their third-party vendors have access to and assign it a risk value, such as high, medium, or low. Then depending on the risk value that a vendor has access to, a risk management strategy would be developed and applied. The higher the risk level, the more stringent the risk management requirements are for that vendor (e.g. monthly walkthroughs or weekly risk reporting), whereas lower risked vendors may only be required to provide a Risk IQ assessment (Martin, 2019). Rockwell Automation CISO, Dawn Capelli, went on to explain that she, as a result of evaluating her third-party vedor's risk, would provide a risk rating of that vendor to offer to other companies. This effectively allowed other companies to see how a third-party vendor was graded so that they could make smart vendor choices, and it likewise encouraged the vendors to conduct secure practices (Capelli, 2019).

Conclusion

For an organization with as many resources and as large as Verizon to suffer from third-party vendor breaches, there is no doubt that companies of all sizes across the country are just as susceptible, if not more so. It is essential for the protection of their customers and the survival of their business that companies start taking seriously the threat of their third-party vendor's security practices. Implementing a security framework to draw down the risk of the organization's internal information security is only the start. From there, reaching out to third-party vendors to understand their data management practices and conduct data risk assessments is as essential as locking the storefront door at the end of the day. No matter how stringent an organization's security measures are, anyone who also has access to their data must have equally stringent security implementations. After all, the chain is only as strong as its weakest link.

References

Cimpanu, C. (2018, November 16). *AWS Rolls Out New Security Feature to Prevent Accidental S3 Data Leaks*. Retrieved from www.zdnet.com: https://www.zdnet.com/article/aws-rolls-out-new-security-feature-to-prevent-accidental-s3-data-leaks/

Cybersecurity Legislation 2019. (2019, April 9). *Cybersecurity Legislation 2019*. Retrieved from www.ncsl.org: http://www.ncsl.org/research/telecommunications-and-information-technology/cybersecurity-legislation-2019.aspx

Frenkel, S. (2015, August 24). *These Two Companies Are Helping Governments Spy On Their Citizens*. Retrieved from www.buzzfeednews.com.

Holst, A. (2019, June 21). *Number of Subscribers to Wireless Carriers in the U.S. from 1st Quarter 2013 to 3rd Quarter 2018, by Carrier (in Millions)*. Retrieved from www.statista.com: https://www.statista.com/statistics/283507/subscribers-to-top-wireless-carriers-in-the-us/

Kelly, M. (2018, November 16). *Survey: Third-Party Data Risk Still a Mess*. Retrieved from www.radicalcompliance.com.

Martin, T. (2019, June 19). 2019 Norwich University Cyber Security Summit. (W. C. Harris, Interviewer)

Moraetes, G. (2018, January 26). *Choosing the Right Security Framework to Fit Your Business*. Retrieved from www.securityintelligence.com: https://securityintelligence.com/choosing-the-right-security-framework-to-fit-your-business/

Newman, L. (2017, July 15). *Blame Human Error for WWE and Verizon's Massive Data Exposures*. Retrieved from www.wired.com: https://www.wired.com/story/amazon-s3-data-exposure/

O'Sullivan, D. (2018, December 12). *Cloud Leak: How a Verizon Partner Exposed Millions of Customer Accounts*. Retrieved from www.upguard.com.

8

CCLEANER

By: Mary Knapp

If there is one thing to take away from the CCleaner hack of 2017, it's that supply chain protection is unbelievably important. A compromise of a part, most certainly can affect the whole. Although it wasn't known that this was part of the issue when the CCleaner hack was first discovered, it came to light after a deeper dive into what really happened at Piriform in 2017.

Ironically, CCleaner software was designed to help scan and clean computer files on a computer to help protect its user, but the malicious software inserted into the CCleaner download file in the 2017 hack actually gathered user information to send back to the hackers. The code gathered computer information such as IP address, computer name, software on the computer, and information about attached networking equipment. Interestingly, no sensitive personal information such as social security number or bank/credit card information was gathered or sent (Bradford, 2017). Also of note, the software would only execute on a 32-bit computer, and if the user who was logged in did not have admin rights, the execution of the code ceased immediately (PC Risk, 2017). This limitation would mean that any company who did not give their individual users admin rights over their machine would not have been affected by this payload.

The CCleaner hack of 2017 affected over 2 million users during a distribution of legitimate CCleaner software that contained a malicious payload. Everyone who downloaded CCleaner between August of 2017 and September of 2017 was affected. However, the original hack took place months before the release of the tainted software. Hackers had to first gain access to a system as an initial breach point, and then spread their reach further once inside and undetected on the network.

In March of 2017, a CCleaner developer's unattended workstation was first attacked, which was connected to Piriform's network. At that time, Piriform was CCleaner's parent company. Hackers were able to gain remote access to that workstation after stealing the developer's credentials in a data breach that happened prior to this incident. Once they had access to the workstation, they then installed a VBScript. After this, they attackers moved on to breach other computers on the same network and opened a backdoor so that they could insert more malicious code at will. Second stage malwareware was also inserted onto the workstation that served as the original breech point. Everything done thus far went completely undetected.

In April of 2017, the third stage of the attack took place when a customised version of ShadowPad backdoor software was installed, thus allowing the hackers to insert more malicious code and/or steal information (Khandelwal, 2018). In the IT world, ShadowPad is one of the most well known backdoor attacks in the software supply chain, though patches are readily available to mitigate quickly now.

The attackers altered the CCleaner download to contain their malicious code in the coming months, during which time Avast purchased Piriform and became CCleaner's new parent company. In August, they used the backdoor to upload the altered CCleaner download, which was then distributed until September 13, 2017 when Cisco Talos discovered and notified Avast (Khandelwal, 2018). Updated software was released soon after, though only cloud users and paid users received that software via an automatic update. Users of the free version of CCleaner had to manually update their software to patch their system.

The likely perpetrators in the case of CCleaner is a group from China known as Barium (or in some cases ShadowHammer, ShadowPad, or Wicked Panda) (Staff, 2019). This group seems to be interested in spying rather than trying to focus on profiting from their distributions. They target their systems with keyloggers and try to steal passwords, rather than using tactics like encrypting information for ransom. It's possible, the hackers work this tactic so that they can gain further access into other systems and supply chains. This theory is supported by Barium's hack into the company Asus, which seems to be a result of access gained through an interlink of Asus and CCleaner in the CCleaner attack. (Staff, 2019). Had Barium decided to launch an ransomware attack instead of a spy campaign, the results would have been devastating given the 2.27 million users that were affected (Warren 2017). But their target seemed to be spreading rather than trying to gain immediate profit.

So what did the world learn from the CCleaner hack? As stated before, certainly this attack highlights the importance of a clean supply chain, specifically a software supply chain in this instance. The problem with an attack in a software supply chain is that malicious code may go undetected, and the distribution of that code is often quickly deployed to vast endpoints. When that software comes with a trusted name, users will generally download this affected software without question.

The other takeaway is not only the importance of software updates and patches, but the ability for a software company to push auto-updates to users. There are a lot of arguments both pro and con for an auto-update, but in the case of CCleaner, once a clean download of the software was made available, cloud based users and paid users were protected with an automatically updated version of the software, while the users of the free version of CCleaner were made to uninstall their software, redownload the clean version, and then reinstall the software manually. Obviously, the latter took significantly more time if the user upgraded their software at all. CCleaner's parent company did comment that they are working towards an automated update for their free version users (Peckham, 2017). Either way, both software companies and users should be vigilant when patching and maintaining their systems, not only for the safety of their information, but for the protection of everyone who might be affected by creeping, malicious code.

References

Bradford, A. (2017, September 19). How to protect your device from Avast CCleaner malware. Retrieved from https://www.cnet.com/how-to/ccleaner-was-hacked-heres-what-to-do-next/

Khandelwal, S. (2018, April 18). CCleaner Attack Timeline 'Here's How Hackers Infected 2.3 Million PCs. Retrieved from https://thehackernews.com/2018/04/ccleaner-malware-attack.html

PC RISK. (2017, December 22). Analysis of CCleaner Hack Reveal Tech Giants Targeted. Retrieved from https://www.pcrisk.com/internet-threat-news/11707-analysis-of-ccleaner-hack-reveal-tech-giants-targeted

Peckham, M. (2017, September 18). What You Need to Know About the CCleaner Malware Attack. Retrieved from https://time.com/4946576/ccleaner-malware-hack/

Staff, W. (2019, May 3). A Mysterious Hacker Group Is On a Supply

Chain Hijacking Spree. Retrieved from

https://www.wired.com/story/barium-supply-chain-hackers/

Warren, T. (2017, September 18). Hackers hid malware in

CCleaner software. Retrieved from

https://www.theverge.com/2017/9/18/16325202/ccleaner-

hack-malware-security

9

EQUIFAX

By: Bill Phillips

The purpose of this article is to provide an analysis of the catastrophic breach of Equifax, a national credit reporting agency, and its systems that occurred in 2017. Dr. Cole observes that "a data breach occurs when an adversary or malicious actor takes advantage of a vulnerability within an organization, either a technical or human weakness, and successfully exfiltrates information" (Cole, 2018). The Equifax breach resulted in the disclosure of the personal data of more than half of all Americans (Whittaker, 2018). The analysis includes a description of how the breach occurred and the best practices that should have been used to avoid it. Additionally, lessons that may be learned from the event, as well as the ramifications resulting from the breach are enumerated.

National Credit Reporting Agencies

There are three major national credit reporting agencies (CRAs) TransUnion, Experian and Equifax. These agencies exist to provide data on which companies may make informed risk-based determinations on whether they should extend services to consumers. CRAs collect information about where consumers live and work, whether or not a consumer pays bills on time or have filed for bankruptcy, been sued or arrested. All of this data is aggregated into a single "credit report" which is then sold to "creditors, employers, insurers and others" (N.A., 2018). The companies that are consumers of the credit reports, use the data to determine a consumer's eligibility for credit, jobs and insurance policies. As a CRA, Equifax collected, stored and sold data on Canadian, British and American citizens. "It's a pretty simple business model, actually. They gather as much information about you as possible from lenders, aggregate it, and sell it back to them" (Sweet, 2017).

How the Crime Occurred

The thieves that stole personally identifiable information

(PII) and the sensitive financial information of more than 145

million American citizens, exploited a vulnerability created by a

software flaw to obtain a point of entry into Equifax's systems.

The vulnerability was present in an element of Apache Struts 2, a

tool leveraged by developers to create web applications in Java.

NIST determined the severity of the vulnerability to be a 10,

Critical, the highest severity rating available using the Common

Vulnerability Scoring System (CVSS) as seen in Figure 1 below.

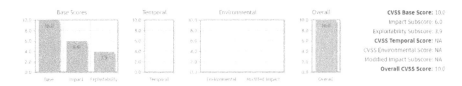

Figure 1. Common Vulnerability Scoring System Calculator Version

3 CVE-2017-5638

Apache Struts Vulnerability

The vulnerable element of the Apache Struts framework

presents in the Jakarta Multipart parser that mishandled files

uploaded to the web server, allowing hackers to remotely run code (Fox-Brewster, 2017). If the Content-Type HTTP header is invalid, an error message is returned. According to Mort, the vulnerability in Jakarta occurs because the "Content-Type is not escaped after the error, and is then used by LocalizedTextUtil.findText function to build the error message. This function will interpret the supplied message, and anything within ${...} will be treated as an Object Graph Navigation Library (OGNL) expression and evaluated as such. The attacker can leverage these conditions to execute OGNL expressions that in turn execute system commands" (Mort, 2017).

The vulnerability in the Apache Struts framework was disclosed on March 7th, 2017. That same day, exploits were available through both ExploitDB and Metasploit, as was the patch to fix the vulnerability. Equifax received notification of the vulnerability from the U.S. Department of Homeland Security's Computer Emergency Readiness Team (CERT) on March 8th but failed to successfully apply the patch to their credit dispute portal.

Criminals first exploited the vulnerability to gain access to the portal on May 13th, 2017. Investigations indicate that in the months following the initial infiltration the first group of hackers handed off control to a more sophisticated team. This new team created more than 30 separate entry points (Riley, Robertson, & Sharpe, 2017) to provide themselves with multiple paths back into Equifax's computer systems should the breach be detected. More importantly the new team was able to exfiltrate data on more than 145 million Americans before the breach was discovered by the Equifax information security department. A breakdown of the quantities and types of information stolen are provided in Figure 2 below.

Name	146.6 million
Birthdate	146.6 million
Social Security Number	145.5 million
Address	99 million
Gender	27.3 million
Phone Number	20.3 million
Driver's License Number	17.6 million
Email Address	1.8 million
Credit Card information	209,000
Tax ID	97,500
Driver's License State	27,000

Driver's License	38,000
Social Security or Taxpayer ID card	12,000
Passport	3,200
Other	3,000

Figure 2. A breakdown from Equifax on how many people were affected by category

According to the prepared testimony of Richard F. Smith before the U.S. Senate Committee on Banking, Housing, and

Urban Affairs Committee; Equifax's information security department became suspicious of traffic associated with the consumer dispute website on July 29th, 2017. A complete time line of the Equifax breach is provided in Appendix A. Smith testifies that the security team continued to monitor traffic and responded by taking the site completely off line on the 30th of July, ending the criminal hack (U.S. Senate Committee on Banking, Housing, and Urban Affairs, 2017).

How the Crime Could Have Been Avoided

Equifax could have prevented the breach entirely if they had simply applied an available patch to a known vulnerability in a timely manner. During his testimony Smith observed, "we now know that the vulnerable version of Apache Struts within Equifax was not identified or patched in response to the internal March 9 notification to information technology personnel" (U.S. Senate Committee on Banking, Housing, and Urban Affairs, 2017). Given revenue of over $3.3 billion with a profit last year of $838.5

million (Finkle & Saxena, 2018), Equifax's failure to properly implement such a fundamental security control is inexcusable.

Equifax chose not to invest in the most basic of security practices. Understanding and managing vulnerabilities as a continuous activity, requires significant time, attention, and resources. The Center for Internet Security (CIS) identifies continuous vulnerability management among the "basic" security controls required for proper "cyber hygiene". Proper cyber hygiene refers to "the basic things that you must do to create a strong foundation for your defense" (CIS, pg. 3, 2018). Equifax had the resources available to address the shortcoming but failed to do so. Newman notes "but Equifax has money, it wasn't like they were on a shoestring budget. It was a decision not to invest here, and that's what kind of blows me away" (Newman, 2017c).

Lessons to be Learned

It is always preferable to learn difficult and costly lessons by observing another's actions and learning from their mistakes or successes. The Equifax breach contains several lessons that may be learned including, vulnerability management, and limiting organizational liability through proper incident response. The degree to which Equifax may be held financially liable for their failure to secure consumer data remains to be seen.

Patch Management

The breach illustrated the importance of a patch management program and the race condition that exists as each new patch is released. The Apache Struts vulnerability provides a near worst case scenario for the cyber defender. In this instance, a working exploit was developed and available the very same day that the vulnerability was disclosed. Responsible disclosure of identified vulnerabilities resulted in the availability of patches on the same day that a vulnerability is disclosed 87 percent of the time. See Figure 3 below.

Even though the patch for the framework was made available in concert with the vulnerability announcement, enterprise environments typically require some time to test a patch against their systems to ensure that it is not disruptive. Patch management programs need to ensure that patching cycles get

shorter so that security gaps are closed in days or weeks, not

months (Knutson, 2017).

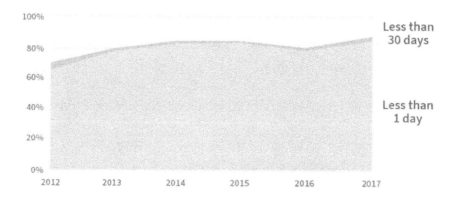

Figure 3. Patch availability for vulnerabilities in all products,

historically (Flexera, 2018).

Limit Organization Liability

Several examples of what not to do in response to security

incident were provided by Equifax during their response. Days

after discovering the breach three of the top executives sold large

blocks of stock totaling nearly $2 million (Isidore, 2017). It is

important to remember that once a security incident has been

identified, every action taken by an organization may be

scrutinized later in court to determine the degree to which it is liable. Organizational liabilities may also be limited to the degree that the organization's response demonstrates their adherence to best practices, is responsible, prompt, and generous. The Equifax response was none of these.

Instead, Equifax sought to maximize the revenue that the incident response could generate through the auto renewal, and billing, of their credit monitoring service after the one-year period that they were providing the service elapsed. The website created to offer the services to consumers impacted by the breach was created outside of the equifax.com domain at *https://www.equifaxsecurity2017.com*. As if that were not bad enough, Equifax then tweeted a URL that was different than the site that the company had created, see Figure 4 below.

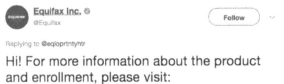

Equifax Inc. @
@Equifax

Follow

Replying to @eqloprtntyhtr

Hi! For more information about the product and enrollment, please visit: securityequifax2017.com. -Tim

3:11 PM - 19 Sep 2017

Figure 4. **Equiphish** – A Tweet from Equifax account directing consumers to the wrong website

This exposed customers and their data to even more harm creating a nearly optimal phishing opportunity for any bad actor. ARS technical detailed additional shortcomings of the site including: "a stock installation of WordPress, a content management system that doesn't provide the enterprise-grade security required; a TLS certificate that didn't perform proper revocation checks; and a domain name that looked like precisely the kind of thing a criminal operation might use to steal people's details" (Goodin, 2017).

Equifax's response has made it abundantly clear that the CRAs have little to no regard for consumer data. This may be due in part, to the fact that consumers are not their customers, rather they are the commodity. These businesses buy and sell consumers data as a raw material to make profit with little to no consideration for the impact that a breach will have on the data owners.

Ramifications

The Equifax breach will impact both consumers and CRAs. While it is clear that the ramifications to consumers will be nothing short of lifelong and profound, one can only hope that the CRAs will be impacted in an equal measure. The Equifax breach spilled the data required for consumers to enter into binding contracts for goods, services, utilities and mortgages. This information is now in the hands of criminals that may at any point in the future monetize the data exposing the consumer to fraudulent charges and contracts executed in their name without their consent.

This lifelong impact to the data owners caused by the negligence of Equifax has created traction for a "systemic reform to the credit oligopoly" (Wieczner & Roberts, 2017). The CRAs that collect, retain and sell consumer information as a commodity are not faced with the same oversight requirements that other industries must endure to ensure security controls are deployed. Bernard observes that the CRAs "are covered by many of the same data security laws that apply to banks. But banks face much stricter oversight, with a team of agencies working together to audit institutions and monitor their compliance. Non-bank companies, like the credit bureaus, generally are scrutinized only after something has gone wrong" (Bernard & Cowley, 2017). This may change if the Data Breach Prevention and Compensation Act (DBPCA) is passed. The DBPCA seeks to force the CRAs to accept several reforms including, a free and easy way for consumers to freeze their credit, mandated penalties against credit reporting agencies, mandated adherence to national technology standards and security frameworks, and a mandate that the FTC establishes an Office of Cybersecurity to perform annual inspections and supervise cybersecurity within the CRAs (Wieczner & Roberts, 2017).

Conclusion

As this article has demonstrated the CRAs are strictly focused on the enormous profits generated by their business model and have little incentive to protect the commodity that they collect and sell, consumer information. The CRAs true customers are the "banks, mortgage providers and marketers to whom they sell that data—business that accounted for nearly two-thirds of Equifax's $3.1 billion in revenue last year" (Wieczner & Roberts, 2017). Without new legislation requiring that consumer data be properly protected, the CRAs will continue with business as usual forcing the consumer to bear the burden of a future data breach. The politicians of both the political parties should act in the interests of their constituents to ensure that the CRAs are forced to adhere to security practices that protect the data of consumers. It will be essential that consumers make their voices heard and demand changes to the credit reporting industry. TansUnion is already preparing for the upcoming battle hiring nine new lobbyist who, according to the company "were enlisted to advocate on issues affecting data security, privacy and cyber-security' "(Neidig, 2017).

References

Alfred, N. G. (2018). A full breakdown arrives of Equifax's massive

data breach. Retrieved from

https://www.cnet.com/news/equifaxs-data-breach-by-the-

numbers-the-full-breakdown/.

Apache Struts: From Bug to Breach | Black Duck Software. (2017).

Retrieved from https://www.blackducksoftware.com/ug-

download/apache-struts-breach

Bernard, T. S., & Cowley, S. (2017). Equifax Hack Exposes

Regulatory Gaps, Leaving Consumers Vulnerable. Retrieved

from

https://www.nytimes.com/2017/09/08/business/equifax.htm

Cole, E. (2018). Online danger: Breach prevention manifesto.

Retrieved from https://secure-anchor.com/

Finkle, J., & Saxena, A. (2018). Equifax profit beats Street view as

breach costs climb. Retrieved from

https://www.reuters.com/article/us-equifax-cyber/equifax-profit-beats-street-view-as-breach-costs-climb-

idUSKCN1GD5C7

Flexera. (2018). Vulnerability review 2018 - global trends.

Retrieved from https://info.flexerasoftware.com/SVM-WP-

Vulnerability-Review-2018

Fox-Brewster, T. (2017). How hackers broke equifax: exploiting a

patchable vulnerability. Retrieved from

https://www.forbes.com/sites/thomasbrewster/2017/09/14/

equifax-hack-the-result-of-patched-

vulnerability/#2deb3ada5cda

Goodchild, J. (2017). Analysis: Why Equifax Breach is So

Significant. Retrieved from

https://www.bankinfosecurity.com/interviews/analysis-

equifax-breach-so-significant-i-3697

Goodin, D. (2017). Equifax sends breach victims to fake

notification site. Retrieved from

https://arstechnica.com/information-technology/2017/09/equifax-directs-breach-victims-to-fake-

notifi cation-site/

Grenier, K. (2016). Dealing with a data breach: Key takeaways

from the Home Depot class action. Retrieved from

http://www.nortonrosefulbright.com/knowledge/publication

s/144326/dealing-with-a-data-breach-key-takeaways-from-

the-home-depot-class-action.

Isidore, C. (2017). Equifax's delayed hack disclosure: Did it break

the law? Retrieved from

http://money.cnn.com/2017/09/08/technology/equifax-

hack-disclosure/index.html

Knight, A. (2016). How Online Marketplace Lenders Benefit From

Reporting Credit Data - Experian Insights. Retrieved from

http://www.experian.com/blogs/insights/2016/02/online-

marketplace-lenders-and-data-reporting/

Knutson, C. (2017). Equifax Lessons Learned. Retrieved from

https://sbscyber.com/portals/0/documents/sbs2017-

equifaxbreach.pdf

Krebs, B. (2017). Equifax Breach: Setting the Record Straight — Krebs on Security. Retrieved from https://krebsonsecurity.com/2017/09/equifax-breach-setting-the-record-straight/

Kurzer, R. (2017). Equifax and beyond: How data breaches shaped 2017 - MarTech Today. Retrieved from https://martechtoday.com/equifax-beyond-data-breaches-shaped-2017-208388

Mort, S. (2017). CVE-2017-5638: Anatomy of the Apache Struts Vulnerability. Retrieved from https://blog.blackducksoftware.com/cve-2017-5638-anatomy-apache-struts-vulnerability

N.A. (2014). How Do Credit Reporting Agencies Get Their Information? | Equifax Finance Blog. Retrieved from https://blog.equifax.com/credit/how-do-credit-repo rting-agencies-get-their-information/

N.A. (2018). Credit Reports and Scores | USAGov. Retrieved from https://www.usa.gov/credit-reports

Neidig, H. (2017). Retrieved from

http://thehill.com/policy/technology/354582-transunion-

beefs-up-lobbying-presence

Newman, L. H. (2017a). Equifax Officially Has No Excuse. Retrieved

from https://www.wired.com/story/equifax-breach-no-

excuse/

Newman, L. H. (2017b). The Equifax Breach Exposes America's

Identity Crisis. Retrieved from

https://www.wired.com/story/the-equifax-breach-exposes-

americas-identity-crisis/

Newman, L. H. (2017c). How to Stop the Next Unstoppable Mega-

Breach—Or Slow It Down. Retrieved from

https://www.wired.com/story/how-to-stop-breaches-

equifax/

Newman, L. H. (2017d). How to Protect Yourself From That

Massive Equifax Breach. Retrieved from

https://www.wired.com/story/how-to-protect-yourself-from-

that-massive-equifax-breach/

NIST. (2017). Common Vulnerability Scoring System Calculator Version 3 CVE-2017-5638. Retrieved from https://nvd.nist.gov/vuln-metrics/cvss/v3-calculator?name=CVE-2017-5638&vector=AV:N/AC:L/PR:N/UI:N/S :C/C:H/I:H/A:H

Office of Senator Elizabeth Warren (2018). Bad credit: Uncovering equifax's failure to protect americans' personal information. Retrieved from https://www.warren.senate.gov/files/documents/2018_2_7_Equifax_Report.pdf.

Riley, M., Robertson, J., & Sharpe, A. (2017). The Inside Story of Equifax's Massive Data Breach. Retrieved from https://www.bloomberg.com/news/features/2017-09-29/the-equifax-hack-has-all-the-hallmarks-of-state-sponsored-pros

Scott, J. (2017). ICIT Analysis – Equifax: America's in-Credible Insecurity – Part One. Retrieved from https://icitech.org/icit-analysis-equifax-americas-in-credible-insecurity-part-one/

Shevlin, R. (2018). Save Us From the Data Breach Prevention and

Compensation Act - Insight Vault. Retrieved from

https://www.crnrstone.com/insightvault/2018/01/10/save-

us-data-breach-prevention-compensation-act/

Sweet, K. (2017). Equifax Collects Your Data, and Then Sells It.

Retrieved from https://www.inc.com/associated-

press/equifax-data-money.html.

Teitler, K. (2017). Did Equifax Wait Too Long to Notify the Public?

Retrieved from https://misti.com/infosec-insider/did-equifax-

wait-too-long-to-notify-the-public

U.S. Senate Committee on Banking, Housing, and Urban Affairs.

(2017). Prepared testimony of Richard F. Smith before the

U.S. Senate Committee on Banking, Housing, and Urban

Affairs. Retrieved from

https://www.banking.senate.gov/imo/media/doc/SmithTesti

mony 10-4-17.pdf

WhiteSource. (2018). How Software Composition Analysis Cloud

Have Prevented the Equifax Breach | Tech Library. Retrieved

from

https://www.informationweek.com/whitepaper/database-security/risk-management-security/how-software-composition-analysis-cloud-have-prevented-the-equifax-breach/394613?gset=yes&

Whittaker, Z. (2018). Here's how the Equifax breach breaks down. Retrieved from https://www.zdnet.com/article/how-the-equifax-breach-breaks-down-by-the-numbers/

Wieczner, J., & Roberts, J. J. (2017). The Equifax Breach Could End the Credit Industry as We Know It. Retrieved from http://fortune.com/2017/10/20/equifax-breach-credit/.

Winkler, I. (2017). What business can learn from the Equifax data breach. Retrieved from https://www.csoonline.com/article/3222882/data-breach/what-business-can-learn-from-the-equifax-data-breach.html

Wolff-Mann, E. (2018). Elizabeth Warren's bill would thrash Equifax for another data breach.

Appendix A

Apache Struts: From Bug to Breach | Black Duck Software. (2017).

10

MAERSK

By: Gene Lilenthal

On June 27, 2017, Maersk was one of many organization to be attacked by NotPetya malware (Maersk, 2018). Forensic analysis by Talos Intelligence showed that M.E.Doc, which is accounting software produced by Ukrainian company Intellect Service, and used by Maersk, was the source of the attack (Talos Intelligence, 2017). The attackers had penetrated Intellect Service's network and obtained "root" access to the server housing M.E.Doc source code, where they inserted back doors into the software. Intellect Service subsequently pushed out the poisoned software as updates to Maersk and other organizations. In this way, adversaries had gained backdoors into organizations' networks. Attackers used the backdoors to deliver the NotPetya payload onto organizations' computers. The U.S. Government concluded that the Russian Federation was behind the attacks as part of the on-going conflict with the Ukraine (White House, 2018). Experts believe Russians targeted Intellect Service since companies in the Ukraine are required by law to use government-approved accounting software, and M.E.Doc has an 80 percent market share (ID Agent, 2017).

NotPetya is a worm that can quickly infect an entire network and destroy infected systems and data (US-CERT, 2017). Once the NotPetya worm was loaded onto the initial Maersk computers having the M.E.Doc software, NotPetya used a variety of different tools to help it spread (Symantec Security Response Team, 2017). NotPetya has a module with Mimikatz, enabling the worm to extract and read hashed or clear-text network administrator credentials running in memory (Thompson, 2017). NotPetya then scanned the subnetwork of the compromised computer(s) for additional Windows computers to attack. NotPetya then used Windows administration tools PsExec and WMIC along with the captured administrative credentials to remotely connect and infect additional computers. It is believed that the attackers chose to use PsExec and WMIC since these are widely used administrative tools, and so their use would have not generated security alerts. To maximum its chances of infecting computers, NotPetya also exploits vulnerabilities associated with SMBv1. After NotPetya got local administrative access onto Maersk computers, the worm rewrote the company's computer hard drives' master boot records. When Maersk computers rebooted, only the malware started up, instead of computers' operating systems. As an extra measure, NotPetya encrypted filesystem tables and files using AES 128-bit encryption. Maersk contained the cyberattack on June 28, 2018 (Maersk, 2017).

Ramifications

NotPetya caused significant damage to Maersk. A computer outage, affecting all business units, occurred around the globe on June 27 (Gronholt-Pederson, 2017). The attack clogged 76 ports run by Maersk, delaying receipt and delivery of containers (Jenson, 2018). Maersk could not receive new shipping orders electronically since the firm had to cut off connections with customers and service providers to avoid infecting others. It took 10 days for Maersk to recovery its technology infrastructure (John Churchill, 2017). The firm had to replace 45,000 workstations, 4,000 servers and re-install 2,500 applications (Snabe, 2018). The total cost to Maersk was between U.S. $250-300 million (Maersk, 2017).

Actions Maersk Should Have Taken Before the Attack

Based on news reports, Maersk had significant security program weaknesses, contributing to the damage NotPetya caused. Maersk could have taken actions before the attack to prevent occurrence or limit damage. Most importantly, the foundation of Maersk's information security program should have been to maintain a strong security culture and a governance program promoted by the board of directors and senior management (FFIEC, Information Security Booklet, 2016, pp. 2-4). With that foundation, leadership should have established an enterprise cyber risk appetite to drive cybersecurity strategies, policies, standards and controls with the stated goal of keeping the level of risk to an acceptable level. Another key function in Maersk's governance program should have been to maintain a continuous assessment of the firm's cybersecurity risk (NIST, 2014). According to the NIST Cyber Security Framework, risk assessments should include identification of foreseeable cyber threats, an assessment of likelihood of occurrence and their impact, an assessment of control effectiveness, and, if applicable, prioritization of efforts to lower risk to an acceptable level. Based on media coverage, it is probable Maersk cyber risk assessments would have identified gaps that the firm could have addressed to prevent or minimize impact from a destructive worm attack:

- Maersk should have blocked outside access to all unneeded ports, including 137, 138, 139 and 445 at their Internet facing firewall and on their internal network (Thompson, 2017). NotPetya required these ports to communicate inside and outside the Maersk network. Thus, blocking them would have prevented loading the malicious payload and the worm's spread. Additionally, Maersk should have disabled SMB on all Microsoft hosts if they were not using this service (US-CERT, 2017). The Center for Internet Security (CIS) notes that restricting ports and services to only those needed is a critical control because it can help prevent exploitation of some vulnerabilities (CIS, 2018).

- Maersk should have applied Microsoft's security patch 4013389 noted in MS 17-010 to remediate SMBv1-related vulnerabilities (US-CERT, 2017). Microsoft released this "Critical" patch on March 14, 2017 (Microsoft, 2017), 106 days before the attack occurred. CIS notes that patching systems is one of the top 5 critical controls because timely, risk-based patching minimizes the window of opportunity for attackers to exploit vulnerabilities (CIS, 2018). The fact that so many Maersk systems were destroyed by NotPetya could indicate Maersk failed to disable SMB or apply the patch.

- Talos advised that any organization with Ukrainian software, or has offices in the Ukraine, should treat these computers with extra caution since they have a history of being targeted by the Russian Federation and Russian-sponsored actors (Talos Intelligence, 2017). CIS recommends that organizations should control and detect network traffic flow between systems with different criticality and trust levels (Center for Internet Security, 2017). Having such a control, may have isolated the NotPetya attack to smaller area of the network. Instead, Maersk had a flat internal network, allowing the worm to cross the network unimpeded (Robert Vamosi, 2017).

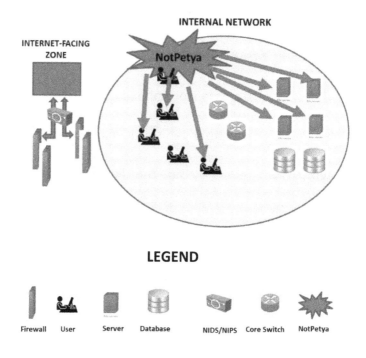

Diagram 1: Flat internal network, i.e. no zones of trust

Based on CIS, Mitre (Bodeau, 2015, pp. 51-52) and FFIEC,

(FFIEC, Information Security Booklet, 2016, pp. 19-20)

recommendations, it is this author's opinion Maersk

should have zoned its internal network by having

Ukrainian operations, critical production systems,

network management systems, general end users, backup

systems, and systems for managing multi-factor

authentication located in separate zones on the internal network. Maintaining firewalls and network intrusion detection systems in front of each zone to monitor, block and alert on unauthorized traffic may have prevented the worm from getting outside the Ukraine Zone and sped the recovery.

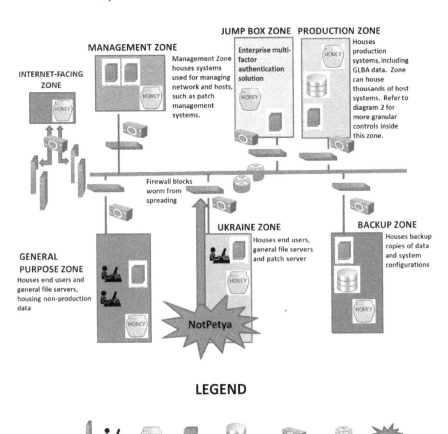

Diagram 2: Resilient zoned internal network

For additional assurance that worm and other attacks are detected, Mitre recommends organizations maintain a honeypot network (Bodeau, 2015, p. 35), which is shown in Diagram 2.

- As recommended by NIST (NIST, 2016, p. 1) and the FFIEC (FFIEC, Information Security Booklet, 2016, p. 33), Maersk should have required multi-factor authentication to access sensitive and critical applications, such as remote administrative access to Windows machines. NotPetya was able to exploit the common weakness that organizations use the same single factor static password to administer many machines.

- Maersk should have had a contingency plan to respond to destructive malware attacks (FFIEC, 2015). Having a documented playbook for this foreseeable scenario would have facilitated response and recovery processes. CIS notes that within Control 10: Data Recovery Capability, organizations need to have the ability to recover systems quickly (CIS, 2018). As it was, Maersk realized after the attack had occurred that the company had no way to remotely set up new systems in masse. As a result, Maersk employees involved in the recovery effort ended up having to go to stores near their headquarters, buy thousands of USB sticks, load each with computer images, and ship them to company locations around the globe. This ad-hoc method caused an unnecessary delay in recovery. A table top exercise of this attack scenario should have revealed weaknesses in using single factor authentication for remote administration, maintaining a flat network, and having an ineffective cyber incident recovery strategy.

Lessons Learned

Maersk, similar to many other organizations, was highly vulnerable to sophisticated, well-resourced cyber-attacks. The attack exposed the immaturity of Maersk's cybersecurity risk management relative to the inherent risk. Additional board and senior management commitment was needed. Going forward, the board needs to build a strong security culture, articulate the cybersecurity risk appetite level, and ensure that appropriate cybersecurity measures are embedded across the firm. To ensure that cybersecurity risk is managed effectively, Maersk needs to maintain a continuous cyber risk management function, which assesses the types risks faced, their probability and severity, and corresponding controls that need to be maintained. Several frameworks, including the NIST Cyber Security Framework, ISO 27001/27002 and COBIT, are internationally recognized sets of security principles that could help guide Maersk in strengthening its cybersecurity program before the next major attack occurs.

Conclusion

The March 2017 NotPetya wiper worm cyber-attack showed Maersk had a number of security weaknesses. The attackers had breached a software vendor's network, and installed back doors into accounting software, which was then pushed to Maersk and other companies as a software update. The attackers used the back doors to load the NotPetya wiper worm into Maersk's network. Attackers designed NotPetya with a number of capabilities to maximize its spread and inflict severe damage. Notable gaps in Maersk's security controls allowed NotPetya to sweep across the firm's network, destroying 45,000 workstations and 4,000 servers. Around the globe, Maersk operations were shut down, costing the firm between U.S. $250 – 300 million. Maersk could have avoided the cyber-attack by deploying a defense-in-depth program informed by continuous risk assessments mandated by management and the board.

References

Batashvili, David (February 15, 2017) *Russia's Cyber War: Past, Present and Future* – EU Observer - https://euobserver.com/opinion/136909 (Batashvili, 2017)

Bodeau, Deborah & Graubart, Richard (September 2011) *Cyber Resiliency Engineering Framework* – Mitre.org - https://www.mitre.org/sites/default/files/pdf/11_4436.pdf (Bodeau, Cyber Resilience Engineering Aid - The Updated Cyber Resiliency Engineering Framework and Guide on Applying Cyber Resiliency Techniques, 2015)

Bodeau, Deborah (March 22, 2018) SP 800-160 Vol. 2: *Systems Security Engineering: Cyber Resiliency Considerations for the Engineering of Trustworthy Secure Systems* – National Institute of Standards and Technology - https://csrc.nist.gov/publications/detail/sp/800-160/vol-2/draft (Bodeau, SP 800-160 Vol. 2: Systems Security Engineeriing: Cyber Resiliency Considerations for the Engineering of Trustworthy Secure Systems , 2018)

Churchill, John (September 14, 2017) *When the screens went black* – Maersk - https://www.maersk.com/stories/when-the-screens-went-black (John Churchill, 2017)

CIS (March 6, 2018) *Control 9: Limitation and Control of Network Ports, Protocols, and Services* – Center for Internet Security - https://www.cisecurity.org/controls/limitation-and-control-of-network-ports-protocols-and-services/ (CIS, 2018)

CIS (March 6, 2018) *Control 3: Continuous Vulnerability Management* – Center for Internet Security - https://www.cisecurity.org/controls/continuous-vulnerability-management/ (CIS, 2018)

CIS (March 6, 2018) *Control 12: Boundary Defense* – Center for Internet Security - https://www.cisecurity.org/controls/boundary-defense/ (Center for Internet Security, 2017)

CIS (March 6, 2018) *Control 10: Data Recovery Capability* – Center for Internet Security -

https://www.cisecurity.org/controls/data-recovery-

capability/ (CIS, 2018)

Coates, Michael (August 31, 2017) *How NotPetya ransomware*

used legitimate tools to move laterally – Techtarget –

https://searchsecurity.techtarget.com/tip/How-NotPetya-

ransomware-used-legitimate-tools-to-move-laterally

(Cobb, 2017)

FBI (July 3, 2017) *FBI Flash: Indicators Associated with*

Ransomware Attack Potentially Modeled After Petya – U.S.

Dept. of Justice Federal Bureau of Investigation –

Infragard.org

FFIEC (February 5, 2015) *Appendix J: Business Continuity Booklet* –

Federal Financial Institution Examination Council -

https://ithandbook.ffiec.gov/it-booklets/business-

continuity-planning/appendix-j-strengthening-the-

resilience-of-outsourced-technology-services.aspx (FFIEC,

2015)

Gronholt-Pederson, Jacob (June 27, 2017) *Maersk says global IT breakdown caused by cyber-attack* – Reuters - https://www.reuters.com/article/us-cyber-attack-maersk/maersk-says-global-it-breakdown-caused-by-cyber-attack-idUSKBN19I1NO (Gronholt-Pederson, 2017)

Hackett, Robert (June 27, 2017) *This Ukrainian Company Is Likely Behind the Ransomware Wave* – Fortune - http://fortune.com/2017/06/27/petya-ransomware-ukraine-medoc/ (Hackett, 2017)

ID Agent (August 3, 2017) *NotPetya – A Threat to Supply Chains* – ID Agent - https://www.idagent.com/2017/08/03/notpetya-threat-supply-chains-across-ukraine/ (ID Agent, 2017)

Jenson, Teis (June 28, 2017) *Cyber-attack hits shipper Maersk, causes cargo delays* – Reuters.com - https://www.reuters.com/article/us-cyber-attack-maersk/cyber-attack-hits-shipper-maersk-causes-cargo-delays-idUSKBN19J0QB (Jenson, 2018)

Maersk.com (August 16, 2017) *Interim Report: Q2 2017* –

files.shareholder.com -

http://files.shareholder.com/downloads/ABEA-

3GG91Y/6181927192x0x954061/7EB88BAD-F1AE-4E86-

9B95-

FF32017D31F9/APMM_Interim_Report_Q2_2017.pdf

(Maersk, 2017)

Maynor, David (July 5, 2017) *The MeDoc Connection* – Talos

Intelligence -

http://blog.talosintelligence.com/2017/07/the-medoc-

connection.html (Talos Intelligence, 2017)

Microsoft (March 14, 2017*) Microsoft Security Bulletin MS17-010*

– Critical: Security Update for Microsoft Windows SMB

Server (4013389) – Microsoft -

https://docs.microsoft.com/en-us/security-

updates/SecurityBulletins/2017/ms17-010 (Microsoft,

2017)

Microsoft (June 27, 2017) *New ransomware, old techniques: Petya adds worm capabilities* – Microsoft - https://cloudblogs.microsoft.com/microsoftsecure/2017/06/27/new-ransomware-old-techniques-petya-adds-worm-capabilities/ (Microsoft, 2017)

NIST (January 10, 2017) *Cybersecurity Framework v1.1* – NIST.gov - https://www.nist.gov/cyberframework

NIST (April 21, 2016) *Best Practices for Privileged User PIV Authentication* – NIST - https://csrc.nist.gov/csrc/media/publications/white-paper/2016/04/21/best-practices-for-privileged-user-piv-authentication/final/documents/best-practices-privileged-user-piv-authentication.pdf (NIST, 2016)

Offensive Security (2018) *Mimikatz* – Offensive Security - https://www.offensive-security.com/metasploit-unleashed/mimikatz/

Skou, Soren (February 9, 2018) *Becoming the global integrator of container logistics* – Maersk -

https://www.maersk.com/stories/becoming-the-global-

integrator-of-container-logistics (Maersk, 2018)

Snabe, Jim Hagemann (January 24, 2018) *Securing a common

future in cyberspace* (World Economic Forum) –

YouTube.com -

https://www.youtube.com/watch?time_continue=491&v=

Tqe3K3D7TnI (Snabe, 2018)

Symantec Security Response Team (October 24, 2017*) Petya

ransomware outbreak: Here's what you need to know* –

Symantec - https://www.symantec.com/blogs/threat-

intelligence/petya-ransomware-wiper (Symantec Security

Response Team, 2017)

Thompson, Iain (June 28, 2017) *Everything you need to know

about the Petya, er, NotPetya nasty trashing PCs

worldwide* – The Register -

https://www.theregister.co.uk/2017/06/28/petya_notpet

ya_ransomware/ (Thompson, 2017)

US-CERT (July 10, 2017) *Alert (ICS-ALERT-17-181-01C): Petya Malware Variant (Update C)* – ICS-CERT - https://ics-cert.us-cert.gov/alerts/ICS-ALERT-17-181-01C (US-CERT, 2017)

Vamosi, Robert (June 30, 2017) *Beyond WannaCry and NotPetya/Petya: What's Next for Enterprises* – Synopsys - https://www.synopsys.com/blogs/software-security/beyond-notpetya-petya/ (Robert Vamosi, 2017)

White House (February 15, 2018) *Statement from the Press Secretary: NotPetya* – U.S. White House - https://www.whitehouse.gov/briefings-statements/statement-press-secretary-25/ (White House, 2018)

11

CISCO SMART INSTALL

By: Mary Knapp

The root of the cyberattack came from the exploitation of vulnerabilities within Cisco's legacy (old) Smart Install protocol (Fingas, 2018). These vulnerabilities led the attackers to being able to, "modify the TFTP server setting, exfiltrate configuration files via TFTP, modify the configuration file, replace the IOS image, and set up accounts, allowing for the execution of IOS commands" (Biasini, 2018). Upon the discovery of the vulnerability Cisco created and distributed a patch to correct the issue but the patch was never fully integrated by the users of the vulnerable routers. (Fingas, 2018) This limited acceptance of the patch caused there to be over 200,000 switches that were at risk around the world, the number varies by source (Fingas, 2018). This wide spread and publicized set of vulnerabilities soon drew the attention of a group of "Vigilante hackers" who wanted to attack Russia and Iran whom they believed were the culprits behind tampering with the United States' presidential election (Cox, 2018).

What the ramifications were

The ramifications of the attack were wide spread affecting the intended targets of Russia and Iran along with some unintended targets to include the United States, China, India, and countries across Europe (Fingas, 2018). The attack hit internet service providers and data centers the hardest causing internet access to be cut off from end users and the defacing of connected computers (Fingas, 2018) (Reuters Staff, 2018) (Cox, 2018). This defacing was not seen on every connected computer but as reported in Iran connected computers showed an image of an American flag with the words, "Don't mess with our elections…." (Fingas, 2018). There were no reports of serious damage being caused by the attack however (Fingas, 2018). It was reported in Iran that the issues were fixed within hours of the attack and there was minimal damage along with no data loss by affected parties (Fingas, 2018). The attackers also claimed to have corrected the vulnerability within switches residing outside the targeted nations but there was no substantial proof given to back up this claim (Fingas, 2018).

Some other repercussions that have occurred outside of the cyber realm were the creation of theories to why the attack was conducted in the first place (Fingas, 2018). The theories that have come about are that the attack was conducted to throw off investigators of the presidential election, or for it to have been just indiscriminate protest to nation states interfering with the elections of other nation states (Fingas, 2018).

How it could have been avoided

There is a number of ways this attack could have been prevented. The biggest way the attack could have been prevented was through ensuring that patches and updates are being made regularly to all an organization's systems, this goes double for legacy systems (Fingas, 2018). The only reason 200,000 plus Cisco switches were in a predicament where they could be attacked in the first place was due to their owners failing to keep them up to date (Fingas, 2018) (Biasini, 2018). The integration of an update review plan for an organization and all its systems would have prevented this attack from occurring (Fingas, 2018). Increasing security practices like upgrading and replacing legacy software would also have taken care of the problem because if there is no legacy system to exploit attackers cannot exploit them (Fingas, 2018). Viewing updates as more than just a nascence would also help towards ensure an organization would have been protected from this attack (Fingas, 2018). Yes it is not ideal to take systems offline for updates but what is better, be offline for a few minutes or a few hours like in this attack (Fingas, 2018)? Listening to warnings of reputable sources like the U.S. CERTs would also have gone a long way to avoid this attack (Biasini, 2018). Listening to reputable sources would have not only given forewarning of the potential attack but also ways to mitigate against those attacks (Biasini, 2018). Having an access control list would have avoided the attack because of how the vulnerabilities work (Biasini, 2018).

If not just anyone has access the attacker would have to take

possession of an account with access before exploiting any of the

for mentioned vulnerabilities (Biasini, 2018). The final method of

how this attack could have been avoided is a mixture of listening

to the suggestions of trusted sources like US CERT and just having

good setting management (Biasini, 2018). For any system

vulnerable to this attack the command no vstack should be run to

prevent the unwanted access (Biasini, 2018).

What are the lessons learned from the attack.

The lessons learned from the attack are straight forward

and easy. An organization must ensure that all of their systems

are up to date and running the most current versions in order to

prevent most compromises (Fingas, 2018). Effective

communication between state entities and those of the private

sector is key (Reuters Staff, 2018). Before and during the attack

Iran failed to both prepare and react in a timely manner due to

there being a "weaknesses in providing information to (affected) companies" (Reuters Staff, 2018). This weakness is something that exists in every state or federal organization due to its inherent nature of information moving slowly due to paperwork and the time it takes for decision makers to see it (Reuters Staff, 2018). This speed bump must be worked around before any further plans or progress can be made. The paperwork and decision makers can be worked around through pushing decision making down to the lowest level and creating an ask for forgiveness environment over an ask for permission. Leaders at the friction point may not always see the big picture but they sure can fix the one they do see. A final note of lessons learned also comes from Iran and how their reaction time was slowed by their new year's celebrations (Reuters Staff, 2018). Someone in a decision making position must always be on to react to the unexpected. If someone, with power, was working at the time of the attack their reaction time to the incidence could have been drastically cut down.

In Conclusion

This attack could have been prevented at multiple times and at multiple levels if only individuals at decision points acted when they should have. As shown in this chapter something as simple as ensuring that patches were up to date and legacy systems are timely replaced could have prevented hours of down time. In our business time is money and you can never get it back. For who conducted the attack I believe it was what all the referenced articles pointed to; a group of "Vigilante hackers" who wanted to make a statement to who they believed were responsible for interfering in the United States' presidential election (Biasini, 2018) (Cox, 2018) (Fingas, 2018) (Reuters Staff, 2018). As a final important note it is dangerous to not be up to date on the current status of warnings and alerts from the producers of the products you use. Chances are from the referenced articles that the reason the attackers were so successful was due to how the entire exploit was pointed out to them by Cisco and they were able to exploit that information in a timely enough manner to commence their attack (Biasini, 2018). If

your enemy has the time to scan through documents for your

weaknesses you should make time to do the same.

References

Biasini, N. (2018, April 5). *Critical Infrastructure at Risk: Advanced Actors Target Smart Install Client*. Retrieved May 16, 2018, from TALOS: https://blog.talosintelligence.com/2018/04/critical-infrastructure-at-risk.html

Cox, J. (2018, April 7). *"Don't Mess With Our Elections": Vigilante Hackers Strike Russia, Iran*. Retrieved May 16, 2018, from MOTHERBOARD: https://motherboard.vice.com/en_us/article/a3yn38/election-hacking-vigilante-russia-iran-cisco

Fingas, J. (2018, April 07). *Global cyberattack targets 200,000 network switches (updated)*. Retrieved May 16, 2018, from engadget: https://www.engadget.com/2018/04/07/global-cisco-switch-cyberattack/

Reuters Staff. (2018, April 7). *Iran hit by global cyber attack that left U.S. flag on screens*. Retrieved May 16, 2018, from REUTERS: https://www.reuters.com/article/us-iran-cyber-hackers/iran-hit-by-global-cyber-attack-that-left-u-s-flag-on-screens-idUSKBN1HE0MH?feedType=RSS&feedName=technologyNews&utm_source=Twitter&utm_medium=Social&utm_campaign=Feed%3A+reuters%2FtechnologyNews+%28Re

12

ETERNAL BLUE

By: Stephanie Invernizzi

It takes a certain degree in applying both skill and knowledge of programming languages, vulnerabilities, and exploits in order to create effective malware. Over the last decade, various experts and companies have estimated that hack attacks cost the worlds economy over $1 trillion per year (Holt, T. 2015. P.96), a number that will maintain its growth so long as the technology world preserves its constant development. This report will present details pertaining to what the EternalBlue exploit is and how it takes over areas of weaknesses. It will also convey some remedial actions that can be taken in order to either become or remain protected against this threat.

Ransomware, a form of malicious software (or malware),

threatens with harm, usually by denying a user access to their

data. The attacker will then demand a ransom from the victim,

"promising" but certainly not always true to their word, to restore

access to the data upon payment. Once the ransom has been

acknowledged users are shown instructions for how to pay an

assailant the requested fee in order to get the needed decryption

key in return. The costs that victims are asked to pay can range

from a few hundred dollars to thousands, and the payments are

more often than not payable to cybercriminals in Bitcoin (Nadeau,

M. 2018). These types of attacks continue to disrupt networks

across the globe, and the growth in both the volume and

sophistication of ransomware remains to be a significant security

challenge for organizations.

The History Behind The Exploit

In 2017, the growing trend of crypto jacking became the new

and preferred on the rise methodology for hackers to utilize.

Crypto jacking, similar to ransomware to some degree, is the unauthorized use of someone else's computer to mine

cryptocurrency (Nadeau, M. 2018). Hackers are able to do this by

either getting the victim to click on a malicious link in an email

that loads crypto mining code onto the computer or by infecting a

website or online ad with JavaScript code that auto-executes once

loaded into the victim's browser (Nadeau, M. 2018). The crypto

mining that can occur with this type of attack is a computationally

intensive process that computers of which are compromising a

cryptocurrency network complete, to verify the transaction

record, which is referred to as the blockchain. Once this part of

the process takes place the digital coins are received in return,

which would imply victory for the hacker (Orcutt, M.2017). So

why is crypto jacking relevant when it comes to the EternalBlue

exploit?

EternalBlue is the name that has been given to the

software vulnerability within Microsoft's Windows operating

system (OS), which was developed by the National Security

Agency (NSA). The exploit was leaked by the Shadow Brokers

hacker group on April 14, 2017, and was used as part of the worldwide WannaCry ransomware attack on May 12, 2017.

While this exploit may have been utilized as a part of the WannaCry ransomware attack, what makes it even more interesting and dangerous today, is that it has been repurposed for a crypto jacking campaign called WannaMine. This new iteration involves injecting malicious JavaScript into vulnerable websites or delivering it via phishing campaigns. Fileless JavaScript variants have been able to embed malicious code into legitimate web pages to compromise visiting devices (Giandomenico, A. 2018). Simply browsing any of the infected sites can enable attackers to hijack central processing unit (CPU) cycles in order to perform crypto mining on behalf of a cybercriminal.

Just How Does it Work?

The vulnerability works by exploiting the Microsoft Server Message Block (SMB) 1.0. The SMB is a network file sharing protocol, which allows applications on a computer to read and write to files and to request services that are on the same network (Microsoft.com). According to Microsoft, the security update that the corporation issued is critical, and due to the fact that this exploit followed the WannaCry attack, the corporation released a rare Windows XP patch after officially ending support for the software in 2014 (Fruhlinger, J. 2017). There are multiple versions of Windows that are vulnerable to EternalBlue, making this exploit even more superior than its initial impact during the WannaCry attack.

In a statement, Microsoft says that "The severity ratings indicated for each affected software assume the potential maximum impact of the vulnerability and the danger is not in the WannaCry ransomware, but rather in the EternalBlue exploit, which has been using the vulnerability in unpatched Microsoft systems to spread the infection to other unpatched computers (Burgess, M. 2017). The EternalBlue exploit has been seen in both the WannCry and Petya ransomware attacks, and the vulnerability can be exploited in a number of ways. When used for WannaCry, EternalBlue was spread through emails, and it has been stated but not entirely confirmed that with Petya, it was spread through a

software update from a Ukrainian Company (Burgess, M. 2017).

Countermeasures

Microsoft's security page that provides an overview of

Service Message Block and which Windows servers it applies to,

details that the following versions of Windows can all be impacted

by the EternalBlue exploit:

- Windows Vista
- Windows Server 2008
- Windows 7
- Windows Server 2008 R2
- Windows 8.1
- Windows Server 2012 and Windows Server 2012 R2
- Windows RT 8.1
- Windows 10
- Windows Server 2016

(Microsoft.com). The versatility of the tool has made it an

appealing workhorse for hackers, and even though WannaCry

raised EternalBlue's profile, many attackers had already realized

the exploit's potential by then (Newman, L. 2018). Knowing that

cybercriminals have already realized the possibilities of this

exploits capabilities, raises and certainly heightens the need to know what defense mechanisms and countermeasures should be implemented and utilized to ensure protection.

Today, one particular countermeasure that has been identified and made public is the help from IT security firm ESET. ESET has created a free tool (EternalBlue Vulnerability Checker) that can be used to determine whether or not the version of Windows that an individual is running is vulnerable to the EternalBlue exploit (ESET.com). The firm has also indicated that the infiltration method used by EternaBlue is not successful on devices that are protected by ESET and one of the multiple protection layer's (ESET's Network Attack Protection module) blocks this threat at the point of entry (ESET.com). In addition to ESET's efforts, the United States (US) Computer Emergency Readiness Team (CERT) (US-CERT), also suggests that organizations follow its best practices related to SMB, such as:

- Disabling SMBv1
- Blocking all versions of SMB at the network boundary by blocking TCP port 445 with related protocols on UDP ports 137-138 and TCP port 139, for all boundary devices.

(US-CERT.gov). While these remediations are able to protect

individuals from the vulnerabilities that this exploit attacks, users

and corporations must recognize the importance of patching and

maintaining routine maintenance protocol procedures to ensure

computers and software are unharmed.

Conclusion

Even though Microsoft has issued updates that fixed the

SMB vulnerability, to this day, there are still many unpatched

machines that reside throughout the world which are susceptible

to this threat, EternalBlue. As indicated in this report, EternalBlue

was not only used in the WannaCry ransomware attack, it was

further developed to aid in the Petya ransomware attack as well

as with the newest form of crypto jacking attacks caused by

WannaMine cryptocurrency malware. A lot of the success in each

of these attacks can come from the lack of knowledge in knowing

what to not click on when browsing the Web or how to maintain

an updated and adequately secure system. As technology

continues to thrive and cybercriminals keep up with the

development of malware and cryptocurrency needs, there will maintain a need to know how to stop or prevent them. The EternalBlue exploit along with all the attacks that it has enabled thus far, highlight the importance of timely patching and the need for a reliable and multi-layered security solution that is able to block any underlying and malicious tool.

References

Burgess, M. 2017. Everything you need to know about EternalBlue. Retrieved from:

http://www.wired.co.uk/article/what-is-eternal-blue-exploit-vulnerability-patch

Burgess, M. 2017. What is the Petya ransomware spreading across Europe? http://www.wired.co.uk/article/petya-malware-ransomware-attack-outbreak-june-2017

Colyer, R. 2017. NSA Exploit EternalBlue is back. Retrieved from: https://www.theinquirer.net/inquirer/news/3025754/nsa-leaked-hack-eternalblue-back-and-powering-wannamine-cryptojacking-malware

Eset. Vulnerability checker. Retrieved from:

https://www.eset.com/us/about/newsroom/press-releases/eset-

releases-eternalblue-vulnerability-checker-to-help-combat-

wannacry-ransomware/

Fruhlinger, J. 2017. Retrieved from:

https://www.csoonline.com/article/3236183/ransomware/what-

is-ransomware-how-it-works-and-how-to-remove-it.html

Holt, T., Bossler, A., & Seigfried-Spellar, K. (2015). Cybercrime

and digital forensics: An Introduction. N.Y.C., NY: Routledge,

Taylor & Francis Group

https://www.technologyreview.com/s/609031/hijacking-

computers-to-mine-cryptocurrency-is-all-the-rage/

Microsoft. Server Message Block. Retrieved from:

https://docs.microsoft.com/en-us/previous-versions/windows/it-

pro/windows-server-2012-R2-and-2012/hh831795(v=ws.11)

Nadeau, M. 2018. What is Cryptojacking? Retrieved from:

https://www.csoonline.com/article/3253572/internet/what-is-

cryptojacking-how-to-prevent-detect-and-recover-from-it.html

Newman, L. 2018. The leaked NSA spy tool that leaked the world. Retrieved from:

https://www.wired.com/story/eternalblue-leaked-nsa-spy-tool-hacked-world/

Orcutt, M. 2017. Hijacking Computers to Mine Cryptocurrency is All the Range. Retrieved from:

https://www.technologyreview.com/s/609031/hijacking-computers-to-mine-cryptocurrency-is-all-the-rage/

Paganini, P. 2017. Retrieved from:

https://securityaffairs.co/wordpress/60629/breaking-news/petya-ransomware-us-cert-alert.html

Smith, M. 2018. 3 Leaked NSA exploits work on all windows versions since windows 2000. Retrieved from:

https://www.csoonline.com/article/3253247/security/3-leaked-nsa-exploits-work-on-all-windows-versions-since-windows-2000.html

13

UKRAINE NOTPETYA

By: Jason Scott

The days of individual or group hacking have evolved into state-sponsored hacking for specified effects. Consider recent news headlines involving Russian government hacking: "The U.K. and U.S. blamed Russian hackers for a campaign aimed at taking control of routers inside government, critical infrastructure and internet service providers, but also within small and home offices"; (Fox-Brewster, 2018) "In a first-of-its-kind advisory, the U.S. and U.K. warned of malicious cyber activity by state-sponsored Russian hackers who are targeting network infrastructure devices"; and (Lee, 2018) "Russian State-Sponsored

Cyber Actors Targeting Network Infrastructure Devices". (US CIRT, 2018)

Russia's attack on Ukraine's power grid is a prime example of how hacking is now used to accomplish gains other than the traditional extortion techniques like ransomware. Although Russia still denies their involvement in the attack, US investigators with Homeland Security and the CIA have evidence that it was Russia behind the cyber-attack on Ukraine's electricity network where they used an updated version of Petya to exploit SMBv1 vulnerabilities. (Noerengerg, 2017)

The Russian's use of a ransomware attack was a ruse to hide their identity as evidenced by the fact that there was no plan to provide a decryption key to unlock the encrypted data. Their (likely) intent was to cause damage to promote their regional dominance strategy and to test their attacks in preparation of future attacks on other countries. (Grachis, 2017)

This attack began on June 27, 2017 whereby the Russians (presumably) attacked several Ukrainian ministries, banks, metro systems and state-owned entities such as their electrical systems with a mock ransomware virus dubbed NotPetya. This attack wiped data from computers not only from the electrical facilities but banks, senior government officials and an airport causing significant disruption of services. The virus also affected systems in Denmark, India and the United States such as the global shipping company, Maersk (Grachis, 2017)

To initiate the attack, the hackers used a technique known as a watering hole attack whereby the threat actors compromise specific (targeted) websites and insert an exploit that results in a malware infection of computers that visit the site. Once the malware is planted in the target machine, it exploits software vulnerabilities on the host to gain access and deliver other payloads such as remote access trojans, spyware or other malware such as ransomware. (Abendan, 2013) In this situation, they used the NSA's stolen EternalBlue exploit that takes advantage of SMB1 vulnerabilities to propagate malware to other systems very quickly.

The attack appeared to be a variant of the Petya (ransomware) attack but without a kill switch that would keep if from spreading rampantly across the internet and without making the decryption keys easily available that would allow the decryption of data once it was encrypted. There was a decryption key, but it was placed on an email server that quickly identified its signature and shut it down; obviously a farce to make is seem like a typical ransomware attack. Couple these nuances with its drive-by or watering hole capability where it could be spread across the internet, led to the birth of NotPetya. (Bay, 2017)

The initial attack vector was a Ukrainian accounting software, M.E.Doc, used extensively by Ukrainians to help process taxes. The hackers were able gain access to a poorly configured and outdated FTP server that allowed them to inject the malware into the company's update server that laid the ground-work for the widespread propagation of the virus. (Brandom, 2017) Every system that applied the update, installed and propagated the malware that spread like the proverbial "wildfire" across the internet.

Not public at the time but Cisco's incident response team identified a web shell [http://www.me-doc[.]com[.]ua/TESTUpdate/medoc_online.php] with a timestamp of May 31 14:45 2017 revealing a slightly modified version of the open source PHP webshell PAS. Once decrypted, they were able to confirm the threat-actor had stolen M.E.Doc root privileges and made modifications for the webserver that routed traffic through a proxy. (Basini, 2017) Unfortunately, it was not known at the time what the attackers were doing but does confirm the attack vector was a direct cause of poor security.

Once the systems were infected, they spread laterally across the internet to infect other systems with the same SMB1 vulnerabilities and continued to spread infecting systems in Ukraine but around the world and almost crippling shipping giant, Maersk.

This malware made use of several tools to aid its movement throughout networks, infecting as it went. It used a modified version of Mimikatz to extract network admin credentials from machines' running memory and then using PsExec and WMIC to further infect even more machines, expanding exponentially. It was able to spread to domain controllers where it scanned subnets and even used DHCP to identify target hosts where it quickly spread and continued the propagation. (Thompson, 2017)

The software was able to extract administrator credentials from RAM that allowed it to encrypt files using AES 128 encryption and even rewrite local workstation's hard drive's master boot record to where only the malware starts when the machine reboots, rather than Windows; this is what allowed it to display the ransom note. To that end, it was virtually impossible to actually receive a decryption key as there was not enough information provided in the ransom note that would allow the key to be generated assuming it would have been available.

(Thompson, 2017)

The cost of NotPetya will likely never be fully known but The White House named NotPetya as the costliest cyber-attack in history. There is no accurate way to completely estimate the damage, but estimates are in the billions of dollars around the world even though the attack was targeted at the destabilization of Ukraine. This attack destroyed thousands of computers, terabytes of private and government data, and twice caused the first-ever hacker-induced blackouts in the Ukraine.

"Bricked" systems, lost systems, down-time and extensive recovery efforts for the Ukraine are not the only costs associated with this attack. It paralyzed global companies such as Merck, Maersk, FedEx and many smaller companies across Asia, the Americas and Europe where the price tag is estimated in the hundreds of millions of dollars. (Greenberg, 2018) According to Maersk's chairman, the "NotPetya attack totally destroyed our computer network". They had to replace 45,000 PCs, 4,000 servers and 2,500 applications that were responsible for running

operations for their 20,000 fleet (ship) network. As Maersk

handles 20% of the world's trade, this attack affected trade for

most of the world for approximately 10 days. (Olenick, 2018)

Although financial costs associated with an attack are

significant, human well-being is the most important aspect to

consider. Not conclusive enough for all experts to agree, but

NotPetya has been associated with power outages in the Ukraine.

The ramifications of these kinds of attacks on supervisory control

and data acquisition (SCADA) systems have the potential to cause

death and wide-spread panic. Consider the situation where

thousands or hundreds of thousands of people are without

electricity in January where the temperatures in some areas are

sub-zero. Also consider the fact that there could be coordinated

attacks where attackers bring down electrical grids but also fuel

transport systems that cause a shortage of fuel so that backup

generators could not be used. This would leave emergency

management, first responders and even hospitals without power with devastating results.

As mentioned earlier, the root cause of this extensive crime is simply poor security practices. It began with M.E.Doc and their lack of security, first on their FTP server and then other servers and applications that led to the propagation of the malware. Next the fault lies with each organization that was compromised; patches and security best practices were in place at the time that would have protected their systems or at least minimized the spread.

The number one protection mechanism against viruses, worms, trojans and other malware is still to simply patch systems to the most current patch level. (Francis, 2017) In this situation, Microsoft released MS 17-010 in October of 2016, 8 months prior to this attack. This is not to say that patching would have completely stopped this attack as no patching solution is perfect, but it would have had a substantial affect the number of hosts it infected.

Many companies continue to maintain flat networks with little or no network segmentation with physical devices such as routers or virtually with VLANs. According to 24BY7 Security, segmentation of networks with authentication could also help slow down or decrease the avenues available for malware to spread. These types of technical measures help increase the security posture of an organization by authenticating and limiting network traffic. It also provides them the mechanism needed to block specified traffic such as the SMB traffic associated with NotPetya.

Cybercrime is not going away and there is no one single way to protect our digital ecosystem. The lessons learned from this event are nothing new; good security hygiene matters. (Zorz, 2017) This applies from end-user to the Chairman. Fancy machine learning technologies, firewalls, artificial intelligence, SIEMs, and extensive endpoint detection and response (EDR) implementations are great tools in the process but they are just that, tools in the "security shed" that must be coordinated in conjunction with user training, patching and architecture; they must all work together in tandem to create a barrier to attack.

References

Abendan II. (February 13). Watering Hole 101. Retrieved May 18, 2018, from https://www.trendmicro.com/vinfo/us/threat-encyclopedia/web-attack/137/watering-hole-101

Bay, S. (2017, November 06). NotPetya: A Targeted Attack on Ukraine. Retrieved May 18, 2018, from https://www.thecipherbrief.com/notpetya-a-targeted-attack-on-ukraine

Beardsley, T. (2017, August 11). Petya-like Ransomware Explained | Rapid7 Community. Retrieved May 16, 2018, from https://blog.rapid7.com/2017/06/27/petya-ransomware-explained/

Biasini, N. (1970, January 01). The MeDoc Connection. Retrieved

May 18, 2018, from

https://blog.talosintelligence.com/2017/07/the-medoc-

connection.html

Bisson, D. (2017, June 28). NotPetya: Timeline of a Ransomworm.

Retrieved May 16, 2018, from https://www.tripwire.com/state-

of-security/security-data-protection/cyber-security/notpetya-

timeline-of-a-ransomworm/

Brandom, R. (2017, July 03). Ukranian company that spread Petya could

face criminal charges for vulnerability. Retrieved May 18, 2018,

from https://www.theverge.com/2017/7/3/15916060/petya-

medoc-vulnerability-ransomware-cyberattack

Fox-Brewster, T. (2018, April 17). UK And US Accuse Russia Of Hacking

Home Routers In Global Cyberattacks. Retrieved May 18, 2018,

from

https://www.forbes.com/sites/thomasbrewster/2018/04/16/russi

a-accused-of-hacking-network-infrastructure/

Francis, P. (2017). Security Think Tank: Patching is vital and

essentially a risk management exercise. Retrieved May 18,

2018, from

https://www.computerweekly.com/news/450421649/Securit

y-Think-Tank-Patching-is-vital-and-essentially-a-risk-

management-exercise

Grachis, G. (2017, November 30). A look back at cybersecurity in

2017. Retrieved May 15, 2018, from

https://www.csoonline.com/article/3239405/data-breach/a-

look-back-at-cybersecurity-in-2017.html

Greenberg, A. (2018, February 15). The White House Blames

Russia for NotPetya, the 'Most Costly Cyberattack In History'.

Retrieved May 18, 2018, from

https://www.wired.com/story/white-house-russia-notpetya-

attribution/

Greenberg, A. (2018, February 15). The White House Blames

Russia for NotPetya, the 'Most Costly Cyberattack In History'.

Retrieved May 18, 2018, from

https://www.wired.com/story/white-house-russia-notpetya-

attribution/

Nakashima, E. (2018, January 12). Russian military was behind 'NotPetya' cyberattack in Ukraine, CIA concludes. Retrieved May 16, 2018, from

https://www.washingtonpost.com/world/national-security/russian-military-was-behind-notpetya-cyberattack-in-ukraine-cia-concludes/2018/01/12/048d8506-f7ca-11e7-b34a-b85626af34ef_story.html?noredirect=on&utm_term=.3582a3580 2e9

Network segmentation - protect from ransomworms like WannaCry & Petya. (2017, July 03). Retrieved May 18, 2018, from

https://24by7security.com/network-segmentation-protect-against-ransomworms-wannacry-petya/

Ng, A. (2018, February 15). US, UK say Russia behind 'most destructive' cyberattack ever. Retrieved May 15, 2018, from

https://www.cnet.com/news/uk-said-russia-is-behind-destructive-2017-cyberattack-in-ukraine/

Noerenberg, E. (2017, June 30). NotPetya Technical Analysis |

LogRhythm. Retrieved May 18, 2018, from

https://logrhythm.com/blog/notpetya-technical-analysis/

Obeck, S. (2016). The Importance of Good Security Hygiene.

Retrieved May 18, 2018, from

http://www.isaca.org/chapters2/jacksonville/events/Docume

nts/The%20Importance%20of%20Good%20Security%20Hygie

ne%2011-17-2017.pdf

Olenick, D. (2018, January 26). NotPetya attack totally destroyed

Maersk's computer network: Chairman. Retrieved May 18,

2018, from https://www.scmagazine.com/notpetya-attack-

totally-destroyed-maersks-computer-network-

chairman/article/739730/

Smith. (2018, April 17). Russia is hacking routers in global cyber

attacks, US and UK warn. Retrieved May 18, 2018, from

https://www.csoonline.com/article/3268908/security/russia-

is-hacking-routers-in-global-cyber-attacks-us-and-uk-

warn.html

Thomson, I. (2017, June 28). Everything you need to know about the Petya, er, NotPetya nasty trashing PCs worldwide. Retrieved May 16, 2018, from https://www.theregister.co.uk/2017/06/28/petya_notpetya_ransomware/

Zorz, M. (2017, March 08). Why cyber hygiene is vital for the security of your organization. Retrieved May 18, 2018, from https://www.helpnetsecurity.com/2017/03/08/cyber-hygiene/

14

CELLEBRITE

By: Manny Bamba

Forensic analysis has its place for investigating, finding and preserving evidence for resolving potential legal issues. It can also become a double edged sword for unsuspecting users, celebrities and other public figures out there who can become targets for information and other data theft. Cellebrite, an Israeli company which is a purveyor of those types of services and tools find itself in the shoes of the usual frond end victims. In other word, the hacker has been hacked. Essentially, a hacker provided Motherboard a tech portal with a large stash of customer information, databases contents among others amounting to about 900 GB of hacked Cellebrite Data. As known, Cellebrite is one of the most popular and leading companies in the mobile phone hacking industry or ecosystem. According to Cellebrite,

UFED Pro Series (Universal Forensic Extraction Device) is its

comprehensive lab solution to deliver digital intelligence by

uncovering the most data from the "widest" variety of devices,

applications, social media and cloud-based sources. This digital

dragnet is used to harvest data from multiple sources. Essentially,

it targets users by exploiting the important tenants of information

assurance such as Confidentiality, Integrity and Availability among

other security services provided by these information attributes.

As partly understood, UFED incorporate phone cracking

technologies that supposedly target crime suspects or help

resolve legitimate investigations. However, these tools can also be

used for nefarious purposes when they fall into the wrong hands

such as malicious users, state actors for intelligence collections

and other cybercriminals. Understandably, Cellebrite is believed

to be popular with US federal and state law enforcement agencies

as well. Equally, surveillance driven authoritarian regimes also

favor greatly this type of technology for an effective control of discordant voices among their own citizens and political

opponents as revealed by the hacked data.

As presented by the tech site Motherboard, which first

received the breached 900 gigabytes of data by the hacker, the

anatomy of this cyber attack revolves around the disclosure of

Cellebrite customers basic contact information of the registered

users and hashed passwords on its old system. Cellebrite also

confirmed the breach to BBC and acknowledged that it had

recently detected "unauthorized access" on an external web

server. However, interestingly for an unexplained reason or

perhaps by restraint for his professed ideal, the hacker did not

distribute online the included data which appears to be evidence

files from seized mobile phones and logs from Cellebrite devices.

Reputation wise, Cellebrite is tight lipped about its link to

government agencies such as the FBI with BBC report (BBC, 2016)

suggesting that the firm worked with the FBI in an attempt to

hack the iPhone used by San Bernardino killer Syed Rizwan

Farook. Moreover, the firm also acknowledged that one of its tools can extract and decode data from the iPhone 5C which is purportedly to be of the same model used by the suspect. Further report in the Yedioth Ahronoth newspaper also showed that Cellebrite, a subsidiary of Japan's Sun Corp, signed a data forensics contract with the FBI in 2013. Structurally, Cellebrite UFED is viewed as a suite of tools that may be leveraging some open source code as noted by Jonathan Zdziarski, a forensic scientist due to some potential similarities between iOS related code and tools created and used by the jailbreaking community (Vice, 2017). Incidentally, the motivation of the alleged hacker seems to be line with that of an hacktivist or social justice warrior. Portraying his intent and motivation in an online chat with Motherboard, the hacker said that " we are lurching toward a more authoritarian society" where the surveillance state becomes the predominant force to the detriment of civil liberties. For that reason, the hacker further suggests that "it is important to demonstrate that when you create these tools, they will make it out" in the larger ecosystem. Operationally using these tools in the field of hacking, this Cellebrite main product, the Universal

Forensic Extraction Device (UFED), usually comes as a small laptop

size device which is capable of pulling SMS messages, emails, and

other data from thousands of different mobile phone models.

In perpetrating the hack, the attacker claimed to have

extracted the targeted data from a remote Cellebrite server

containing UFED images as source despite the encryption which

he managed to bypass. Additionally, the ripped and decrypted

content also incorporated a fully executable Python script set that

could be readily use to exploit targets according to the hacker

notes in a README file accompanying the data dump. As he

exposed the Cellebrite compromise, the hacker took a step

further by posting links to the data on Pastebin. Moreover, as if to

establish the authenticity of the data source in the hack many of

the directory names were upended with "ufed" along the related

or target phone types such as Samsung or BlackBerry.

Analytically, by presenting its tools as an application suite,

questions can be raised whether this Cellebrite forensic

applications is merely a collection of best of breed from the larger ecosystem of hacking community tool boxes. Even if many of these tools were independently developed, there seemed to be for example some sign of adaptation to a number of configuration files referencing Geohot (the well iPhone hacker)'s limera1n a jailbreaking software based on analysis by researchers in Vice report. The potential effect of these types of similarities or adaptations perhaps coincidental or intentional could weaken or shorten a company resilience to attack and may explain the compromise such as the one Callebrite was target of. As understood, in hacking environment, attribution can be a difficult and protracted process. In the case of Cellebrite hack, allegations are abound that the company straight up ripped off tools from open jailbreaking community that are being leveraged in its commercial product and the jury is still out on that one.

Subsequently, evaluating for a larger point, Cellebrite suffered a cyber attack on part of its server infrastructure hosting his customer data. The hacker exposed information relating to its customers along with their hashed passwords. Furthermore, the hacker managed to disclose the data despite the protective services of encryption that the company had implemented on its UFED images stored on the targeted servers. Incidentally, Cellebrite is in business of forensics, gathering data for intelligence and legal purposes among others. However, in that role hackers and other hacktivist consider these undertaking by the company as an antithesis to civil liberties ideals therefore worthy of attack as a legitimate target. As such, some hackers view Cellebrite as an enabler of surveillance state and authoritarian regimes around the world stifling dissent and other forms of civil or political protest. However, based on the computer law such as the US Computer Fraud and Abuse Act (CFAA) the hackers don't get to pick and qualify their targets as legitimate or illegitimate. For this reason the Cellebrite hack is still considered and constituted an unauthorized access or a potential attack on data belonging to a third party to which the attackers were not authorized and had no ownership of the underlying

information.

References

Baraniuk, Chris. "Phone-Cracking Firm Cellebrite Hacked." *BBC*

News, BBC, 13 Jan. 2017, www.bbc.com/news/technology-

38607670.

Cox, Joseph. "Hacker Steals 900 GB of Cellebrite Data." *Vice*, VICE,

12 Jan. 2017, www.vice.com/en_us/article/3daywj/hacker-

steals-900-gb-of-cellebrite-data.

15

WANNACRY

By: Steven F. Stalker

The 2017 WannaCry Ransomware cyber attack impacted companies and individuals in more than 150 countries, including government agencies and multiple large organizations globally (Bossert, 2017). The malware can run in as many as 27 different languages requesting a ransom of .1781 Bitcoin, which is roughly $300 U.S. (US-CERT, 2017). Organizations affected by WannaCry range from the National Health Services (NHS) of England to the Renault-Nissan auto manufacturer, which halted production in some areas (Langde, 2017). The infected computers' data became encrypted and a ransom message from the hacker demanded payment within three days or the cost would increase (Langde, 2017). Anyone who refused to pay would eventually lose access to their files and information stored in them (Langde, 2017).

Some WannaCry victims received ransom demands, but paying

those demands did not unlock their computers (Bossert, 2017).

Individuals, industry and government were affected and the

consequences were beyond economic.

The Eternal Blue Vulnerability

WannaCry is far more dangerous than other common

ransomware types because of its ability to spread itself across an

organization's network by exploiting a critical vulnerability in

computers running MS Windows. The vulnerability was labeled,

"ETERNALBLUE SMB" and was patched by Microsoft in March

2017 in their "Microsoft Security Bulletin MS17-010 – Critical"

(Microsoft Support, 2017). It is widely suspected that most

Windows users either didn't take the update serious or became

complacent when installing the necessary patch and as a result, the

WannaCry Ransomware attack was able to exploit the SMB

protocol on Windows machines that remained vulnerable (Langde,

2017). The vulnerability, hereafter referred to as, "Eternal Blue",

was released online in April 2017 in the latest of a series of leaks

by a group known as "the Shadow Brokers", who claimed they

stole the data from the Equation cyber espionage group (CERT-MU, 2017).

Journalist Rohit Langde provides a technical explanation of the Eternal Blue SMB vulnerability in his article, "WannaCry Ransomware: A Detailed Analysis of the Attack" (Langde, 2017). Langde states,

> Eternal Blue is a leaked NSA exploit of the SMB protocol in Microsoft Windows that is used to propagate the malware in affected systems. Eternal Blue leverages a technique called pool grooming—which is a type of heap spray attack on kernel memory structure. Targeting vulnerable Windows systems, it injects a shellcode that enables the attacker to use the IP address of the machine to directly communicate with the SMB protocol (Langde, 2017).

Without user interaction, WannaCry runs a script to check for a tool called "Double Pulsar" to verify if it is installed and running on the system (Langde, 2017).

Double Pulsar is a backdoor implant tool that was also developed by the National Security Agency (NSA) and it bypasses the authentication measures of a system and creates a backdoor to allow remote access (Langde, 2017). This brings us to a unique characteristic of WannaCry. The malware uses Eternal Blue for the initial exploitation of the SMB vulnerability and if successful, it then implants the Double Pulsar backdoor and uses it to install the malware (CERT-MU, 2017). If the exploit fails and Double Pulsar is already installed, WannaCry proceeds to install its ransomware payload (CERT-MU, 2017). As was the instance with the WannaCry ransomware cyber attack, the Eternal Blue SMB vulnerability within the MS17-010 software patch provided the hackers with the ideal remote code execution vulnerability to exploit.

The WannaCry Exploit

Wannacry is not just a malware that scans internal ranges seeking a place to spread, rather, it is also capable of spreading based on vulnerabilities it finds in other externally facing hosts across the Internet (CERT-MU). WannaCry leverages the capability to scan heavily over Transmission Control Protocol (TCP) port 445 (e.g. Server Message Block/SMB), spreading similar to a worm, compromising hosts, encrypting files stored on them, then demanding a ransom payment in the form of Bitcoin (CERT-MU, 2017). Once the malware is on a system, its worm capability attempts to spread further through SMB (CERT-MU, 2018). The first thread scans hosts on the Local Area Network (LAN) and the second thread is created 128 times and scans hosts on the wider Internet (CERT-MU, 2018). The remote code execution vulnerabilities existed in the way that MS SMB 1.0 server handles certain requests and the attackers successfully exploited this vulnerability and gained the ability to execute code on the target servers (Microsoft Support, 2017).

The United States Computer Emergency Readiness Team (US-CERT) conducted an analysis of three files, all of which were confirmed as components of the WannaCry ransomware campaign (US-CERT, 2017). The US-CERT analysis is valuable in understanding the functionality of WannaCry. For example, US-CERT states, "The first file is a dropper, which contains and runs the ransomware, propagating via the MS17-010/EternalBlue SMBv1.0 exploit. The remaining two files are ransomware components containing encrypted plug-ins responsible for encrypting the victim users files" (US-CERT, 2017). The

WannaCry dropper is a malicious PE32 executable that attempts to connect to a hard-coded Uniform Resource Identifier (URI) (US-CERT, 2017). If a connection is established, the dropper will terminate execution and if the connection fails, the dropper will infect the system with ransomware (US-CERT, 2017).

When executed, WannaCry is designed to run as a service with parameters (US-CERT, 2017). For example, during runtime, the malware determines the number of arguments passed during execution (US-CERT, 2017). If the arguments passed are less than two, the dropper proceeds to install itself (US-CERT, 2017). Once installed and running, the dropper attempts to create and scan a list of IP ranges on the LAN and attempts to connect using User Datagram Protocol (UDP) ports 137, 138 and TCP ports 139 and 445 (US-CERT, 2017). If a connection to TCP port 445 is successful, the dropper creates an additional thread to propagate by exploiting the Eternal Blue vulnerability (US-CERT, 2017). The dropper then extracts and installs a PE32 binary, which has been identified as the ransomware component of WannaCry (US-CERT, 2017).

Another interesting element of the WannaCry exploit is the highly publicized kill switch domain. This kill switch domain (e.g. iuqerfsodp9ifjaposdfjhgosurijfaewrwergwea.com) was included within the WannaCry script to halt execution if it could connect with a hostname (Langde, 2017). However, since the domain was not registered, the attack continued to execute and spread (Langde, 2017). Former cyber security researcher Marcus Hutchins became an overnight hero when he discovered kill switch in the WannaCry script (Langde, 2017). Hutchins discovered that before WannaCry infected a system or demanded the ransom message, the script made a request to the domain name: iuqerfsodp9ifjaposdfjhgosurijfaewrwergwea.com (e.g. kill switch domain) (Langde, 2017). Coincidentally, Hutchins learned the domain was not registered, so he registered the domain name for $10.69 at NameCheap.com and directed it to a sinkhole server he hosted in Los Angeles, California (Langde, 2017). The rapidly spreading WannaCry ransomware attacks suddenly stopped and according to a tweet from @actual_ransom, the three Bitcoin wallets received around 256 transactions amounting to $76,233.26 USD (Langde, 2017). After careful investigation, in December

2017, the United States publicly attributed the massive WannaCry cyberattack to the government of North Korea (Bossert, 2017).

Effective Countermeasures

Prevention is the most effective defense against ransomware and each individual and organization maintains the responsibility to take precautions for protection (DOJ, n.d.). The speed and success of the WannaCry ransomware should serve as a continuous reminder of the importance of keeping systems updated and patched. Effective countermeasures to protect against ransomware attacks begin with identifying outdated and/or vulnerable software and updating or replacing entirely. Additional countermeasures may include:

- Uninstall or disable unnecessary services and protocols. Malware attacks often exploit these services and protocols as an attack vector (Landge, 2017).

- Run regular penetration tests against the network, no less than once a year (US-CERT, 2017).

- Enable strong spam filters to prevent phishing emails from reaching the end users and authenticate in-bound email

using technologies like Sender Policy Framework (SPF),
Domain Message Authentication Reporting and
Conformance (DMARC), and DomainKeys Identified Mail
(DKIM) to prevent email spoofing (US-CERT, 2017).

- Develop, institute, and practice employee education
  programs for identifying scams, malicious links, and
  attempted social engineering (US-CERT, 2017).

- Ensure anti-virus and anti-malware solutions are set to
  automatically conduct regular scans (US-CERT, 2017).

- Test your backups to ensure they work correctly upon use
  (US-CERT, 2017).

- Scan all incoming and outgoing emails to detect threats and
  filter executable files from reaching the end users (US-
  CERT, 2017).

Conclusion

The stability of the Internet and the security of our
computers are vital to free and fair trade and the fundamental
principles of liberty (Bossert, 2017). Therefore, it is important for
organizations and individuals that value these principles to assume

a more proactive approach in defending against ransomware attacks. The speed and sophistication of WannaCry was truly impressive and everyone should use this catastrophe to learn from. Despite Microsoft issuing their vulnerability patch to prevent these exploits from occurring two months prior, many information technology professionals waited until it was too late to update their software, and in effect, their systems were compromised. The number one take-away from this report is to update your systems whenever possible. Additional proactive measures should include backing up your data regularly; test your backups; ensure your backups are not accessible from local networks; and develop mechanisms for effective training and continued education.

References

Bossert, T. (2017). "Press briefing on the attribution of the WannaCry malware attack to North Korea". The White House, Infrastructure & Technology. Retrieved from https://www.whitehouse.gov/briefings-statements/press-briefing-on-the-attribution-of-the-wannacry-malware-attack-to-north-korea-121917/

CERT-MU. (2017). "The WannaCry Ransomware". Computer

Emergency Readiness Team of Mauritius. Retrieved from

http://cert-

mu.govmu.org/English/Documents/White%20Papers/White%

20Paper%20-

%20The%20WannaCry%20Ransomware%20Attack.pdf

DOJ. (n.d.) "How to Protect Your Networks from Ransomware".

Department of Justice. Retrieved from

https://www.justice.gov/criminal-ccips/file/872771/download

Langde, R. (2017). "WannaCry Ransomware: A detailed analysis

of the attack". Techspective, Home, Security, APT (Advanced

Persistent Threats). Retrieved from

https://techspective.net/2017/09/26/wannacry-ransomware-

detailed-analysis-attack/

Microsoft Support. (2017). "MS17-010: Security update for

Windows SMB server: March 14, 2017". Retrieved from

https://support.microsoft.com/en-us/help/4013389/title

US-CERT. (2018). "Alert (TA17-132A): Indicators associated

with WannaCry Ransomware". United States Computer

Emergency Readiness Team. Retrieved from https://www.us-

cert.gov/ncas/alerts/TA17-132A

16

CONCLUSION

While there were many cybersecurity incidents in 2017, we believe these 14 were the most important to report. Probably the most significant are the theft of the NSA's and CIA's hacking tools. We learned that both agencies have significant cyber operations and do not always disclose vulnerabilities they discover in commercial software.

Over the past two years the significant reporting of cybersecurity incidents has hopefully raised the awareness of the average person to the serious threat of cyber-attacks. The lessons learned from these cybersecurity incidents: Be sure to back up your data. There are many free cloud providers such as Google Drive, DropBox and Microsoft Onedrive; Implement two factor authentication on your online accounts. Most providers now offer SMS text on your cell phone as a second form of authentication.

Thank you very much for reading our book. We hope you learned more about the serious threat of cyber-attacks and will help spread the word to be safe online.

ABOUT THE EDITORS

Thomas S. Hyslip is currently the Resident Agent in Charge of the Department of Defense, Defense Criminal Investigative Service (DCIS), Cyber Field Office, Eastern Resident Agency. Prior to joining the DCIS in 2007, Dr. Hyslip was a Special Agent with the US Environmental Protection Agency, Criminal Investigation Division, and the US Secret Service. Throughout his 20 years of federal law enforcement, Dr. Hyslip has specialized in cybercrime investigations and computer forensics. Dr. Hyslip has testified as an expert witness on computer forensics and network intrusions at numerous federal, state, and local courts.

Dr. Hyslip is currently a faculty member at Norwich University within the Master of Science in Information Security & Assurance program. Dr. Hyslip received his Doctor of Science degree in Information Assurance from Capitol College in 2014. Dr. Hyslip previously obtained a Master of Science degree from East Carolina University and a Bachelor of Science degree from Clarkson University. Dr. Hyslip holds numerous industry and government certification including the Certified Ethical Hacker (C|EH), NSA-IAM, and SCERS from the Federal Law Enforcement Training Center.

Rosemarie A. Pelletier is the Program Director for the Master of Public Administration and Master of Science in Information

Security & Assurance programs at Norwich University. Dr. Pelletier has several years of experience in education, public policy, and real estate. She has been teaching in Virginia for 15 years in the classroom and for about 10 years online, where she wrote and developed courses and chaired dissertation committees. Dr. Pelletier was the president and founder of a company responsible for the identification, research, and development of projects suitable for construction by the formation of a public-private partnership.

Dr. Pelletier served as the Secretary of the Virginia State Technology Council where she advised the Executive and Legislative branches on technology policy issues. She chaired the Transportation Technology Advisory Panel in writing the Transportation Technology Blueprint for the Commonwealth of Virginia. She was appointed by Governor George Allen to the Joint Committee on Technology and Science to study and advise on technology and science policies. Appointed by Governor Mark Warner, Dr. Pelletier served on the statewide speakers bureau to address transportation funding issues throughout the Commonwealth. She combines her knowledge and experience in technology policy with her education in public policy and public administration to bring the best of both worlds to Norwich University.

At George Mason University, she earned her Bachelor of Arts in English and Philosophy, her MPA, and began her Ph.D. work. She then went on to the University of Baltimore to receive her Doctorate in Public Administration, specializing in policy and project implementation.

George J. Silowash was named Chief Information Security Officer (CISO) for Norwich University in December 2016. Previously, he was a cybersecurity threat and incident analyst within the CERT® at the Software Engineering Institute (SEI), a unit of Carnegie Mellon University. He has over a decade of experience in the information technology field, including systems administration and information security. His latest work involves developing technical controls using open source software to counter data exfiltration attempts by malicious insiders. Other areas of interest include privacy and security, digital forensic investigations, and critical infrastructure security. Before joining CERT, he was an Information Systems Security Officer for the United States Department of Justice, National Drug Intelligence Center. He was also a systems administrator for a healthcare company prior to working in the Federal government. He holds a master of science in information assurance from Norwich University and is a certified information systems security professional (CISSP).